Dress Sense

Dress Sense

GUILD PUBLISHING LONDON

MARY GOSTELOW

© Mary Gostelow Enterprises 1985
First published 1985

This edition published 1985 by
Book Club Associates
by arrangement with
B. T. Batsford Ltd

CONTENTS

1 Dress Sense *is for women of all ages and with different lifestyles (drawing Su Quek).*

What this book is about

'In the future, I think, garments for women will be tubes around which you drape belts and other accessories. You have a short tube, a long tube, whatever . . .'

These are the thoughts of Iwan Tirta, the Jakarta designer best known for his superb batiks but with an extensive knowledge of dressing worldwide.

Yes, *Dress Sense* shows where clothes are going. It also shows you where *you* are at the moment. You may be young, old, big, small, city or country based. You may be working, you may be studying, you may have a hectic social life, you may stay at home... Whatever you do and wherever you are, this book will help you to plan the clothes that are best for your lifestyle, with the minimum of effort and expense and the maximum enjoyment and effect.

Fashion implies constant updating and attention to the latest fads that might be utterly impractical for real life. In earlier times, fashion was determined and set by only a minute percentage of society.

Dress, by contrast, is a practical interpretation of what is to be worn and how the various items together constitute the whole (the *wardrobe*). As fashion editor Suzy Menkes comments, dress today 'is made democratically for women who lead various lives' (*The Times*, 15 May 1984).

Dress means that the *person*, and not what she is wearing, is the essential factor. The art of dressing well requires confidence, experience and style, so that clothes become an extension of the wearer rather than being the dominant feature.

One of the chief guidelines to dressing today is to *feel comfortable* at all times. Gone are the eras of constricted and impossibly tight hems.

Cyril Kern, Chairman of the British Fashion Council, a Council Member of the British Knitting and Clothing Export Council, and Chairman, too, of the Reldan Group (Reldan, Ditto and Sheridan Barnett), believes strongly that the average woman of today is much better off than her predecessors:

> Never before has there been an age where women have dressed across the fashion spectrum in clothes that suit them. You will find a woman of 60 plus, if she is active and looking and feeling good, in the same clothes as a 35-year-old and this gives women a much greater opportunity of looking good longer.

This book, therefore, includes information for all age groups. And it includes a whole chapter on the importance of health and beauty. 'Looking good', says Cyril Kern, 'covers a wide sphere, including obviously health, body, make-up and *lastly and most importantly, clothes.*'

You should try to plan ahead so that you can forget completely about what you are actually wearing. Suppose you have put together a co-ordinated outfit for an important occasion. You know you look good. Try to ignore such problems as a skirt hem coming down – unless, of course, the calamity needs such urgent attention as spot removal treatment or is as drastic as a broken zip that reveals nearly all.

How to find your way around the book

Dress Sense is divided into seventeen chapters. You may want to read the book through from cover to cover or simply to turn to the sections in which you are most interested. The index is the key to the whole.

This is your book. There are places for you to write in your own favourite names and ideas. In the last section of the book you will find a place to write in your personal details (no-one need see what you have written!). You may even like to attach, where relevant, swatches of your favourite fabrics.

It *is* a personal book. It is written from my point of view and you will meet, in *Dress Sense*, many of my friends – designers and others involved with dressing.

2, 3 *One of the chief guidelines to dressing today is to feel comfortable at all times; these variations on a simple 'one size' cut are by Su Quek.*

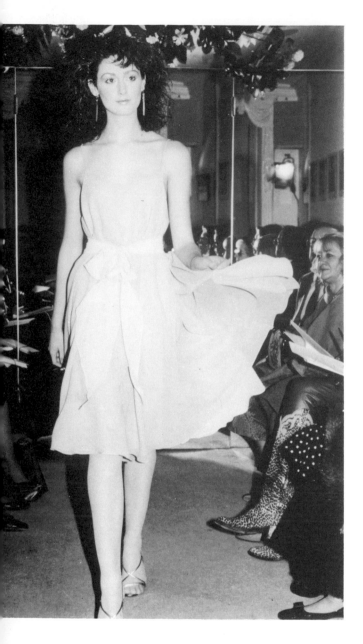

4 *Any dress should be worn with confidence (dress by Emanuel, make-up Barbara Daly, hair John Frieda, photograph David Bache).*

I am indebted to Diana May, who has done a considerable amount of the research and without whose help this book would not have been possible.

I should also like to thank particularly, for their help in many different ways, Wendy Lees, Margaret Rice and Martin Gostelow, and also: Aquascutum and Mary Phillips, Barbara Attenborough Associates and Clare and Nick Attenborough, Gillian Hutcheon and Joanne Howorth; Shirley Barnette; Burberry and Mary Coomes; Cathay Pacific Airways and David Longmuir; The European Commission for the Promotion of Silk and Rosalind Woolfson; Gucci and Jacky Gee; The Home Laundering Consultative Council and C. Bellingham-Smith; The Hong Kong Trade Development Council, Hilary Alexander and Godfrey Malig; The Inter-Continental Hotel, London, and Mary Gunther; The International Wool Secretariat; Lancôme and Susi Jenkins; Neeni Krishna, Diana Landsberg, Margery McKean, Lee Rosati, Kate Stone, Sheila Tuffley and the many others whose names appear in the following text.

CHAPTER 1

How they do it

Who do you have to be, to be well dressed?

Frankly, *anyone* can be well dressed if they spend time – and spend what money they have – wisely. You do not have to pay a lot to be chic – you should simply try not to make mistakes.

One day at lunch Diana May, who helped me substantially with this book, and I, compiled our own 'world's best dressed list'. Some of the people we know, some are famous, but all are *suitably dressed* for their lifestyles.

This was our list, in no particular order:

Linda Evans (who looks good on the set of 'Dynasty' as well as when she publicizes the Spa at Bonaventura in Florida)

HRH The Princess of Wales (sometimes)

Livleen Sharma (high fashion in Delhi)

HM Queen Elizabeth The Queen Mother

Mackay Crampton (Malibu pizzazz)

HM Queen Noor of the Hashemite Kingdom of Jordan

Patty Teo (Singaporean designers' delight)

Nancy Kissinger

Lady Romsey

Moira Stewart (she makes such interesting news)

Sally Noel

Why not do as we did? Next time you are with a girl friend, compile a 'well dressed list', of those you know as well as those you do not, but would perhaps like to meet.

Some of the people on our list are marvellous designers' clothes-horses and it is known who has been responsible for which outfit. Among the Princess of Wales' favourite designers, for instance, are:

Jasper Conran

Bruce Oldfield (designer of that famous off-the-shoulder blue evening dress)

Benny Ong (who works a lot in silk)

Arabella Pollen (young Sloane Ranger favourite, once backed by entrepreneur Naim Attallah)

Other 'best-dressed women' *themselves* put together a look which does not necessarily reflect any particular designer. Frankly, nothing looks as artificial as someone who is dressed from top to toe (including all accessories) by the same House; to see someone looking like an advertisement for a particular designer smacks of 'Nouveau'.

The well-dressed person is not always the one whose clothes you notice. Walking along Piccadilly one day, Diana and I passed a 'fright' whom we shall always remember. Spikey hair topped a lop-sided T-shirt on top of a dirty undershirt and, below, there was a contrasting mini-skirt from which emerged her too-thick legs. We shall certainly remember her, but she would never go in our 'best-dressed' list.

By contrast, one rainy Sunday we went for lunch to the Carpenters Arms in the Somerset countryside not far from Ilchester. One of the waitresses would have received full marks in any dress test. She was up-to-the-minute, with excellent grooming – and we shall certainly go back there again to eat!

The best-dressed woman has to be *consistently* well turned out.

Sally Noel is nearly 5ft 11in., but although some of her friends jokingly say she is 'all legs', she herself says that it is her neck that is long. She can wear more or less anything – and any colour.

Her wardrobe is filled with clothes of all colours of the rainbow, some patterned and some plain. Like many of the best-dressed women, she buys cleverly and some of her outfits last for years without 'dating'.

'I love clothes, I always have', she says. 'I love texture, colour and design. I am a romantic: I appreciate beauty and quality.'

Her wardrobe is a tightly packed selection of trousers, little chiffon dresses, fur jackets, riding and tennis gear, versatile day dresses that go from early morning to evening with several dashes in and out of cars *en route*, and suits that go anywhere, any time. Labels include Guy Laroche and Country Casuals: shoe boxes are marked Bally, Gucci and Bruno Magli.

Now, with her eldest child out of her teens, Sally says she spends more thought on finding garments that co-ordinate, perhaps with some-thing she already has. 'I also find I am now going back to the complete outfit look, with co-ordinating accessories, including tights – it is important, you know, to try to have tights the same colour as your shoes, otherwise the feet appear as two blobs at the end of your legs.

I never think about what I am going to wear until the last mad minute,' she confesses breathlessly. Sally is something of an enigma: she professes not to spend any time at all getting ready for a particular event and yet she never fails to look stunning.

In other words, her formula is to shop cleverly and then combine garments to produce stunning outfits. A best-dressed woman must do this at all times.

We talked to some other women who do care about their clothes and how they look.

Jan Leeming is constantly in the public eye when she reads BBC news and appears at special functions. She always looks immaculately well groomed – as befits the author of *Simply Looking Good*, her book for busy women.

'I do not really have any favourite colours,'

Jan told me. 'I like pastel shades – I like blue, which for a long time I could not wear for technical reasons in front of the camera. The camera does funny things; it cannot cope with strident colours, although I do seem to be wearing quite a lot of red at the moment.

'I am not a keen follower of fashion. You have to be very rich to be a follower of fashion.' I asked Jan if, when appearing 'head and shoulders' in front of the camera, she took as much care with the unseen parts of her as she did with what the viewing public saw.

'Of course I do,' she said. 'I am one of those people who has to have everything matching and correct. A lot of my outfits are dresses or two-pieces. Everything always matches. I like jewellery, but I have to be careful and I cannot wear too much as it is too distracting. I am also not very tall, so I cannot wear big baubles.'

People perhaps do not realize how hard Jan works. One of the problems in being a public person is that she is always on show, whether at work or away from it – though just occasionally Jan can relax in a tracksuit ('I seldom wear trousers otherwise,' she says).

Similarly, Debbie Rix's daily early-morning reading of the news on BBC's 'Breakfast time' means constant public awareness of what she wears. Contrary to what her fans might think, she actually chooses her clothes herself:

> I look after my own clothes for work and simply remember whether I've already worn something that week. I generally wear the kinds of things I like on screen. I prefer separates because you can vary them much more. And personally I would rather have a good casual jacket to throw over most of my wardrobe than a suit which only really works when you wear both bits together. Obviously, if you can afford a suit as well, they do look very smart, but they're not essential. One nice dress is always a must – for the days when you just want to throw something on and look good without worrying about things working together. I usually buy good shoes – cheap ones hurt, no other reason. Lastly, I try to make sure things blend and match – it's cheaper for one thing; most of us cannot afford to wear entirely new colour schemes each day.

Geraldine Rees, who made racing history on 4 April 1982 when she became the first woman to complete the gruelling Grand National, has different clothing problems. Those involved in any sport on a professional basis obviously have to adapt their wardrobes to their physical lifestyles.

6 *A best-dressed woman cleverly combines garments to produce stunning outfits (silk dress with tie-dyed panels, designed and made by Maria Cornejo of Ravensbourne College of Art for the Dylon Students Fashion Competition).*

I first met Geraldine at the Woman of the Year lunch and I asked her how she managed to retain her femininity in a life that involves mucking out stables and riding three lots of horses each morning.

> I do not often have time for make-up except a little mascara, but I wear pearl earrings the whole time. On racing days I always try to wear an outfit which is especially feminine, and if my hair gets untidy – which is quite often – I tuck it into a jaunty peaked cap.

Femininity is an important feature in dressing well. Martine Borgemeister, who works for Laurent-Perrier champagne, says:

> I believe one should take advantage of, or use, one's femininity and I am sure that most of the men in France prefer that way of thinking. I really believe men prefer women in skirts, although I think trousers are all right – but trouser suits are rather severe. On the whole French women are very clothes conscious (and the men seem to take notice) – and they seem to spend a fair amount of money in this way.

On the other side of the English Channel, Diana May went to visit Barbara Hardwick, only woman director of Weight Watchers UK. This is her report:

Barbara laboured for years at $12\frac{1}{2}$ stone (175lbs) until she became a member of the first Weight Watchers class in Britain. She knows what fat people feel, and, as she says, 'People on diets can be boring!'

She is a lover of natural fabrics and a great believer in simple uncluttered styles. Her wardrobe contains a range of formality from a long-sleeved black sequin jacket to a highly versatile khaki tracksuit. Dark colours look particularly dramatic with her silver-grey hair, and she also sometimes complements her colouring by wearing grey and slate blue to match her eyes. She loves knits, and she finds that polo- or boat-necks seem more flattering than round necks; she often buys shirts with collars or bows or some other emphasis at the neck. Lately she has decided that cap sleeves are no longer for her; as years pass her weight fluctuates only slightly but seems to shift about a bit!

She goes for names like Frank Usher, Parigi and Jaeger, and she sometimes buys at Laura Ashley and Wallis. She enjoys shopping, regularly checking the sales with her daughter Julia. She buys when she sees something that is really

right – like a silver-grey crepe dress – even if it will not be worn immediately.

She tries always to have three pairs of high-heeled shoes (navy, wine and grey at the moment) and some low styles (currently black, beige and black-and-grey), and good, though not necessarily matching, handbags.

Her clothes are carefully hung on padded hangers and covered in cotton bags made from old nightdresses. The garments are frequently dry-cleaned and professionally pressed.

When she travels on business (mainly to the States, Germany or Sweden) she always takes the following: a good French black skirt, two silk shirts (one frilly black, one coloured), a knitted or fabric waistcoat, knitted jacket, a bikini for swimming or private sunbathing, one or two kangas to wear over the bikini, plenty of underwear and glasses. She has an emergency pack of toiletries and underwear in her hand baggage.

(If you want to know more about Weight Watchers, look in your telephone directory for details of your nearest local branch.)

Everyone, of course, is to some extent in the public eye. I went to visit Nicola Clarke, 30, who works several days a week with her husband, a leading Humberside businessman. She makes several work trips with him each year and they go to the Roger Taylor Tennis School in Val do Lobo, Portugal.

Home is a large rambling Georgian manor house, now completely redecorated by Nicola herself. She has two busy sons, James (six) and Henry (four).

In her own relaxed and understated way, Nicola advocates *advance planning* when it comes to her clothes. She decided, for instance, that she needed a 'special dress' to wear to summer weddings. Several months before she actually needed the outfit, she talked to her mother, who saw a pattern in *Vogue Pattern Book* that she said she would like to make for her. Nicola – who is herself now turning her sewing talents away from curtains to clothes – bought the required amount of fabric in Scunthorpe market.

Her mother made up the outfit – and Nicola asked a friend, who conveniently owns several shops, if she had any ideas for a hat. Fortunately the friend had seen something, from Kangol, and she ordered it for Nicola. Admittedly, the hat cost nearly twice as much as the dress (excluding her mother's labour) but, with advance plan-

7 *A keen sports enthusiast may well have a voluminous wardrobe of 'special gear'; these workout clothes were sketched in Singapore by Su Quek.*

ning, the finished outfit looks high couture. Because it is devoid of any obviously 'high fashion' pointers such as mandarin collar or deep V-neck, and because the skirt is a classic and always fashionable length – mid-calf – the outfit should last for years.

Nicola leads such a varied life that her clothes must be versatile. She wore her mother-made outfit, without the hat, to York races.

Similarly, she owns a marvellously versatile collection of sweaters, including several knitted by herself and two identical plain navy ones (one lambswool 'for every day' and one cashmere 'for best'). She wears all these with jeans at home but with navy culottes for work.

Navy and red are her favourite colours. One of her best-loved garments, now several years old, is a pair of red linen trousers from Le Painty – 'terribly expensive at the time'. They go with a red-and-white-striped silk top, a basic cream pussy-bow shirt, or with one of her sweaters. 'I never travel without these trousers – I feel *comfortable* in them.'

One advantage of living in the country is that she is personally known in her favourite shops. Nicola can take clothes home to try on and feel if they *are* really comfortable. 'Another good thing is that friends who own shops tell me when their sales are on – I buy all my shoes, for instance, from two specific shops – and they also suggest things to me.'

She has other advantages besides having a skilled dressmaker for a mother. She has excellent colour sense – and she is a perfect size 10 (for more expensive clothes) or 12 (for less expensive items) and her weight never changes, thanks no doubt to tennis several times each week and lots of riding. She also has opportunities of shopping overseas, say T-shirts in Portugal and real leather handbags for a few pounds in Majorca.

She rarely shops in London except at The Sale Shop, where designer clothes are often half price. She goes once a year to Coneys in Boston (the Lincolnshire one), where she has an account. She also acquires some clothes second-hand from her mother – her own cast-offs are sold to friends or passed to jumble sales, though really treasured items, including some dresses, are kept for years.

> I resent spending money on dresses – most of mine actually cost under £20, or my mother made them or they are designer rejects. I love hats and they last for years. I do not need a coat as I never walk anywhere. I have this Mondi ecru jacket and two 'Puffas' quilted jackets, one sleeveless. I do not even own a raincoat, only an umbrella.

Nicola also resents spending money on underwear – she assesses her main extravagances as shoes, which she wears out quickly, and her tennis gear, but, as she says, 'I wear this Kim outfit two to four times every week, and not only on the tennis court.'

This is a good message: clever dressers pay particular attention to what they wear most and, if you happen to be an exercise freak, for instance, it may make sense to have a full range of exciting workout clothes!

Blk trousers
" skirt   navy skirt
" jacket   "
" 'cardi'   "
blk high h.
" med h.

Sea green & black skirt

CHAPTER 2

Body style

You cannot have dress sense without paying attention to the body within . . . Here are some guidelines to help you care for that body.

Your weight

Suggested ideal weights are given at the back of the book.

Weighing yourself should be undertaken methodically:

1 Weigh yourself once a week (not more often) at the same time of day and ideally wearing no clothes.

2 Use the same scales and stand evenly on them: do not lean forwards or backwards.

3 Keep a *note* of your weight.

Overweight?

From a dress sense point of view, being overweight means that you probably do not *feel* your best so you will not *look* your best. It is also more difficult, and more expensive, to have to buy outsize clothes.

How can you change weight?

If you want to *lose weight*, the most important thing to remember is that quick weight loss (e.g. a two-day crash diet) does not only generally mean you quickly put that weight back on again but, even more damaging, your metabolism becomes slower so that in future you need even fewer calories just to maintain your weight.

Sadly, the older woman needs fewer calories* to maintain weight and so more calories need to be omitted to lose weight.

(A calorie is the measure of energy-production of various foods. Items that contain many calories produce a lot of immediate or lasting energy: those that contain few calories produce little energy. Soon the unit 'kilojoules' (kJ) – usually

8 *You cannot have dress sense without attending to the whole body (drawing Su Quek).*

shortened to 'joules' – willl be used instead of calories. 1 calorie (officially a kilocalorie) = 4.2 kilojoules.)

Eat sensibly

Your body needs the following:

(**a**) Carbohydrates for instant energy (from bread, pasta, potatoes etc.).

(**b**) Calcium for bones/teeth (from dairy products).

(**c**) Iron for healthy red blood (from meat, offal, cereals and spinach).

(**d**) Protein, for growth and repair of body cells and tissues (from meat and dairy products and from cereals, nuts, flour, beans, peas and other vegetable proteins).

(e) Vitamins: *A* for growth, sight, and protection against infection (from offal, dairy products, dark green vegetables); *B* for growth, digestion, nerves and the skin (from meat, offal, flour, eggs); *C* for skin, strength (from citrus and other fruits and vegetables); *D* for bones, teeth (from oily fish and fish liver, offal and sunlight).

(f) Fibre, which provides roughage – it aids digestion, helps prevent constipation and seems to stop too much fat and sugar getting quickly into the bloodstream. Fibre can give satisfying bulk to a meal without adding too many calories.

High fibre content is found in: peas, baked and other beans, sweetcorn, baked potatoes and spinach and other leafy vegetables, prunes and all dried fruit, bananas, bran, wholemeal bread and pasta and brown rice.

Medium fibre content is found in: celery and most green vegetables, apples and oranges, cornflakes, muesli, nuts, brown bread.

Low fibre content is found in: lettuce, tomato and cucumber, boiled potatoes, grapefruit, porridge, white bread and rice.

No fibre content is found in: sugar, meat and fish, dairy products.

Suggested further reading: Audrey Eyton, *F-Plan* and *F-Plan Calorie Chart*, Penguin.

Many of the best-dressed people today stick increasingly to a simple diet, following such guidelines as these:

1 Concentrate on *fresh* produce – fruit, salads and vegetables (including all potatoes except chips, crisps or fried), go for seafood, white fish and chicken, skimmed milk and cottage cheese, wholegrain breads and bran, and drink as much water as you can.

2 Exercise restraint when it comes to such foods as bacon, sausages, salami, eggs, red meat, oily fish, full-fat cheeses, thick creamy soups, coffee and tea (which both contain caffeine), salt (which may lead to high blood pressure) and white breads.

3 Bring out iron self-discipline when it comes to cakes, pies, creamy desserts, sugar, sweets, chocolate, preserves, butter and full-fat margarine, meat fat, mayonnaise, any fried potatoes, snacks, spirits.

For a healthy body eat regularly

Eat three to four meals well spaced throughout the day. Try to establish regular mealtimes from one day to the next. Do not skip a meal, especially breakfast (the old advice to 'breakfast like a king, lunch like a lord and dine as a pauper' is still good to follow) and try to avoid between-meal snacks.

Always try to get up from a meal thinking you could eat a little bit more. Try to limit alcohol – and drink *lots of water* at all times of the day.

Posture

Model and beauty expert Oleda Baker has to look good, professionally, the whole time. Her recipe for success is proper diet combined with exercise and *posture*.

She suggests that you begin every day with this posture exercise. Stand, ideally in front of a mirror, with your feet parallel to each other and a few inches apart and arms by your side. Press evenly on the ball of each foot and tighten the muscles in the front of your thighs. Slowly draw your buttocks tightly together and, equally slowly, stretch your spine and draw the shoulder blades together, taking care not to tilt your chin or lift your shoulders.

Skincare

Barbara and Clare Attenborough create skincare products for Boots. I asked them for tips for looking after skin:

> When you are young, it is quite understandable that you do not like to think too far ahead! It is nice to be able to spend your money now rather than invest it in the hope that it will be worth more in years to come. The same thought processes are often applied to skincare. If you have a good skin now you may well think that there is no need to spend time and money until later. Skincare, however, is one area where the old adage 'prevention is better than cure' is absolutely right.

What is skin?

When you consider that the total area of skin on your body is about eighteen square feet, you would think we would be more inclined to treat it with the respect we give to other major organs of the body. Skin is, in fact, one of the most hardworking and complicated systems. First and foremost, it is a protective device, designed to retain moisture and warmth for the well-being of all that lies beneath it.

There are three main layers: the epidermis (the skin we actually see), the dermis (where we find sebum) and the sub-dermis (mainly fatty tissue). Within are sebaceous and sweat glands, hair follicles, vital nerve endings, over 3,000,000 skin cells – and about 20% water. Skin cells are constantly dying and being renewed and this process takes about 17 to 23 days. The sebaceous glands produce sebum, which goes into the hair follicles or 'pores' of the skin and gives a protective and softening covering to the epidermis. If insufficient sebum is produced there is a dry, flaky appearance on the epidermis.

Why do skins differ?

Your skin has its own peculiarities or idiosyncrasies. Just as some people eat a lot and never get fat, so some have better skin than others. It is to a great extent the way you treat it that causes the differences. If you are always eating cakes, sweets, fried foods and drinking sweetened drinks, you cannot expect your skin to be the same as that of someone who avoids all these things and eats plenty of fresh fruit and vegetables and drinks good, plain unadulterated water.

Environment (central heating, air-conditioning and pollution) should also be taken into consideration, as should life habits (heavy drinking, smoking, rushed or missed meals and a hectic pace). All take their toll on the skin.

But we are not killjoys. With the right skincare products and perhaps just a little moderation in diet and pace of life there is no reason why your skin should not look, feel and be perfectly smooth, clear and fresh-looking.

Your skin type and how to care for it

Normal skin is fine-textured, matt and smooth, with no visible pores. There is a perfect balance of oil, moisture and acidity. Dry skin tends to be 'tight', with a tendency towards flakiness and tiny lines. Oily skin looks shiny, has open pores, is sometimes blotchy and is prone to spots and blackheads. In combination skin the 'T-zone' (forehead, nose and chin) is oily and the rest of the face is dry. Sensitive skin is very fine and almost translucent. It will often be dry, with a red tone and tiny broken veins.

The tissue test will help you find out what type of skin you have. Press a clean tissue against your cheek – if there are no transparent marks or oily traces at all, then you have a dry skin. An oily skin will make the tissue go transparent and normal skin will leave a slightly oily residue but will not make the tissue transparent.

You will not necessarily have the same skin type throughout your life. Puberty, pregnancy, the menopause, emotional upsets and stress all affect the skin and may change its type from one extreme to the other.

Skincare products

A good cosmetic company produces products which cleanse, tone and moisten the delicate facial skin. Whatever you are doing and wherever you are, you need to attend to these three routines every day, without fail. There should be a trained person to help you choose the right products for your skin type at your local chemist or drug store, department store or beauty shop.

Personally, I find it is better, and easier, to stick to one brand at a time. I know then that the products will be complementary. At the moment I am using all Boots No. 7 Special Collection for skincare (I love the matt glass pots, but I spoon the creams into little unbreakable plastic pots for travelling).

Make-up

Actual *maquillage* – the artistic paint that shows, like lipstick, eyeliner and so on – can be very much a product of current fashion. Colours change amazingly quickly. If you find a lipstick that really suits you, for instance, it is a good idea to 'stockpile', as otherwise, you might find that shade no longer in stock when you next try to buy it.

Janice Kehoe is a press officer for British Home Stores. She says:

A woman doesn't like being caught without having had ample time to 'put her face on', especially first thing in the morning.

Looking good is important, whether you are a housewife or a career girl, bearing in mind that the main reason for wearing make-up is to accentuate your good features.

After the initial planning of an outfit comes the decision of how to choose and apply your make-up. To project yourself and the style of your clothes, take into consideration the main colour of your outfit and choose a similar shade for your eyes.

Make-up for casual dressing must not appear too harsh. Go for a light, healthy look. Use pretty pastel eyeshadows and soft eye pencils, remembering that your eye colours should not look too bold in comparison with your outfit.

A stronger approach is needed when applying make-up for an evening out on the town. Emphasize the eyes with a darker eyeshadow, highlighting the brow bone and lid with a lighter shade. Outline your lips with a soft crayon, making any adjustments to size and shape, then apply the lipstick with

10 *Same girl as in fig. 9, with evening makeup (makeup by Mary Lou, using British Home Stores' Meadow Flower range for day, Eleanor Moore range for the evening, jewellery by Acsis).*

a brush. Add a lip gloss for a glamorous finishing touch.

Experimenting with make-up can be fun and highly satisfying, especially when you see the startling end results cosmetics can produce for you.

9 *Casual daytime makeup for Terrie Tanaka.*

Hair

'Hair does not make the total look but it is an integral part of that look,' says top international hair specialist, Marc Young. Regardless of whether you are a student or a senior citizen, an executive or a home-based mother, it is important that you look after your hair.

If you were to look at one of your hairs under a powerful microscope, you would see that it is made up of three layers: the outer layer (the cuticle), which is an overlapping series of scale-like cells covering the whole hair, the second layer (the cortex) and the inner core (known as the medulla).

When your hair is in peak condition, the cells of the cuticle lie flat and compacted, giving your hair a beautiful glossy shine. If the cuticle is neglected or if the hair dries out, the cells lie haphazardly and the hair takes on a drab, dull look. The cortex gives the hair strength, elasticity, texture and quality; this layer also contains pigment granules which give hair its colour. The exact function of the medulla is not determined.

No two people's hair grows at exactly the same rate but the average rate of growth slows down, with age, to as little as 0.25cm a month. Hair grows at approximately the same speed all over the head.

Marc Young believes strongly that sensible eating will help keep hair in good condition:

In my opinion, high protein foods are best for our hair, and fish, eggs, white meat, milk and cheese will all help keep your hair strong and healthy. Too high an intake of starch, sugar and 'junk' or highly processed food has the reverse effect, particularly on the scalp. People who over-indulge in starchy food, too much alcohol, rich sauces and so on, often end up with scalp and skin disorders (frequently manifesting themselves in dandruff and other scalp irritations) and the quality of the hair will be affected. An insufficient intake of vitamins can also be detrimental to hair, as can heavy drinking and smoking.

As well as paying attention to your diet, Marc Young recommends that you should regularly have your hair cut or trimmed at a qualified salon. Brushing and regular shampooing form the basis of good home hair care. A good hairbrush, ideally with an interlocked series of little nylon tufts that stand above the bristles, should last up to five years: use a wide-toothed tortoiseshell or plastic comb.

I asked Marc for advice about colour and style.

Often people do not give enough thought to whether the tone of the colour they may wish to have will also match their skin and clothes.

Take red, for example. Red can be based on a red tone, a gold tone or even a violet or blue tone – all look red, but with differing tones. If you have clothes in greys, white, khaki and other murky tones and your hair is coloured in gold, copper and chestnut shades, your 'total look' does not appear quite right. It would, however, if your hair was coloured towards purple, mauve and blue tones.

As far as the choice of hairstyle is concerned, think of the hairdresser's point of view ... A client walks in wearing classic clothes, say a nice, neat skirt, simple black sweater and pearls, with hair that looks as if nothing except shampoo and blow-drying has been done to it for six months. She obviously needs a neat, well-tailored and careful hairstyle *within what is fashionable at the time*. By contrast, if the client was wearing high fashion gear, say big, baggy trousers and a floppy jacket, then she could have a tousled look.

The hairdresser must be careful when assessing what kind of style a client really wants. If you are thinking of having a new style, it is helpful for you, as client, to discuss with the stylist whether or not you always look as you do now.

I always advise hairdressers not to typecast clients into age brackets. It is a good idea to adopt the latest hair fashion and adapt it, considering the client's lifestyle and age, in order to improve her appearance.

Suggested further reading: Marc Young, *The book of hair care for you and your family*, Marc Young and Severn House. (Marc Young's address is at the back of the book.)

11 *A well-groomed head of hair is, with makeup, an essential ingredient of dressing well (photograph courtesy Marc Young).*

How you can do it

Julian Morgan says that her mother always told her to 'wear clothes as if you *mean* to'. That is fine, but first you have to know what kind of figure you are and what you need from your clothes.

Assessing your figure

First, you need to measure yourself.

Make sure you will not be disturbed for half an hour. You will need a friend – and pencil and paper and a tape measure.

These are the measurements you should take (and mark on your Private Measurement Notes at the end of the book):

12 *Measure yourself at these given points.*

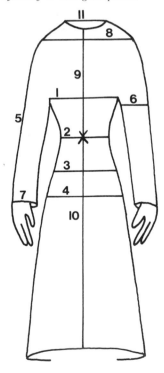

1 Bust (around its most obvious part).

2 Waist.

3 Hip (5″ down from waist).

4 Hip (9″ down from waist).

5 Sleeve length (from natural shoulder to wrist, arm extended).

6 Upper arm.

7 Wrist.

8 Back shoulder width at nape of neck.

9 Back length, nape of neck to waist.

10 Back length, waist to usual hem.

11 Neck.

Now the worst is over!

Wait until you have complete privacy and you can stand, naked, in front of a full-length mirror. Decide what type of figure you really are and draw yourself on top of the shape here (fig. 13).

Be honest. Are you *ectomorph*, *mesomorph* or *endomorph*? (It sounds so much better than saying 'Are you long and lean, muscular and strong – or short and squat?'!).

Some people can wear anything, but, more often than not, 'wearing clothes well' implies a better-than-average figure coupled with good posture. The rest of us may have to make a few compromises!

Consolation dressing

Some people call this 'cosmetic or corrective dressing'. In other words, if you have anything 'wrong' with your body this is how you can cover it up!

Let us start from the top and work downwards. Take the shape of your *face and neck* into account when choosing necklines: if you have a long oval face and/or long neck you will not look good with low, open necklines unless there is a

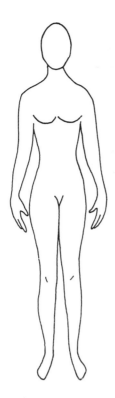

13 *Be honest and mark in, on the outline here,* your own shape. Don't cheat! *No-one need see what you draw. Look at yourself, naked in front of a mirror, and draw what you see on to this figure (it may make it more lifelike if you draw in your hairstyle, as well).*

divider (try drawing in a Victorian choker). If you have a square face and/or short neck you won't be flattered by high, closed necklines. If you have a long oval face and/or long neck you *will* look good with high, closed necklines and if you have a square face and/or short neck you will be flattered by low, open necklines.

If you do not like the look of your neck, you will find that either a short front ruffle or a 'pussy-cat' tie makes a soft cover-up. Surprisingly, a plain boat-neck with diagonal shoulder pleats is also flattering, as the eye is drawn away from the neck itself. Some people deliberately choose a high mandarin collar to 'hide a neck' but I think this shows to the world that there *is* a bad neck to hide.

Now *shoulders*. If yours are sloping or narrow you will look good in extended or padded shoulders and ruffles. If they are wide, avoid extended or padded shoulders or halter necks, which will tend to make you look like a prize fighter. Instead, you should concentrate on raglan necks, with emphasis on lower sleeves (and no shoulder pads) and diagonal lines, with two colours.

14 *Are you long and lean, muscular and strong or short and squat?*

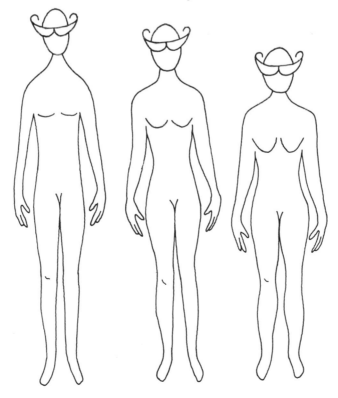

15 *If you have a long neck you can wear a high collar (photograph courtesy Marc Young).*

16
A. *A low open neckline exaggerates a long oval face.*
B. *A high, closed neckline does not flatter a square face.*
C. *A high, closed neckline does look good if you have a long, oval face.*
D. *A low open neckline flatters a square face.*

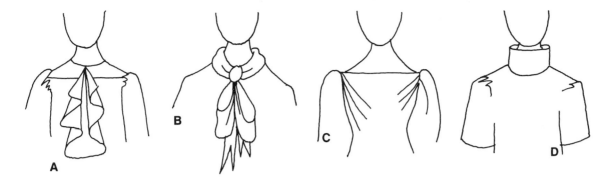

17

A. *A soft front ruffle.*

B. *A 'pussy cat bow'.*

C. *A plain boat shaped neck with diagonal shoulder pleats.*

D. *A high mandarin collar.*

18

A. *If you have wide shoulders you should avoid these.*

B. *You can, rather, wear these.*

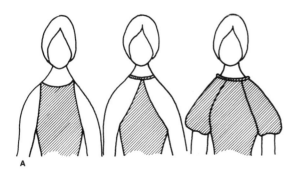

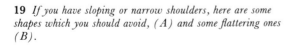

19 *If you have sloping or narrow shoulders, here are some shapes which you should avoid, (A) and some flattering ones (B).*

If your *arms* are too thick or too thin, do not draw attention to them. Avoid sleeveless dresses, short puffed sleeves and anything with too-tight sleeves. Go, instead, for full-length sleeves with some fullness. If you have to wear a sleeveless dress (say in the sun), choose thin spaghetti-type straps. Thin arms look better with thin bracelets: thick arms should complement heavier bracelets.

If your arms are too short, avoid full or puffed sleeves and too much arm jewellery. You might try wearing sleeves slightly longer than most people. If, on the other hand, you have especially long arms, avoid any sleeves that go past your wrist. Full sleeves and bracelets will keep the eye of the beholder 'up' your arm, while long finger-nails, by comparison, would extend the arm even further.

If you feel anything is wrong with your **wrists** – if they are bony or too heavy – avoid drawing attention to them with jewellery. If possible, cover them with full-length sleeves.

If your *back* is your worst feature, avoid drawing emphasis to it. Those with broad backs should steer away from shoulder pads and any tops that are too exaggeratedly tight or voluminous: go instead for well-fitting tops with emphasis on vertical seams and patterns. By contrast, those with narrow backs should avoid too-tight tops, but they will look best in horizontal patterns.

If you have a *large bust*, you may look best in a loose top worn with a tighter skirt. You may feel happy in a larger-than-usual sweater and you certainly look good wearing anything that has soft diagonal lines with emphasis on cleavage. Similarly, you will probably do best to avoid fussy upper sleeves, lighter top and darker bottom, any horizontal stripes that emphasize your bustline and ties that fall over your bust – these may look all right from the front but look at yourself, sideways on, in the mirror!

If you are not sure whether you can wear an obviously *waisted* outfit, try standing nude in front of a full-length mirror and tie a scarf or belt around your waist. If it does not look good round your waist, try it around your bust or your hips. If you are high-waisted you will look best in one colour top and bottom, or in tops that extend below the waist. Sleeve emphasis should similarly not be at waist height. You should avoid obvious belts and a colour change at the waist.

If you have a prominent *tummy*, avoid anything that exaggerates it (e.g. any skirt that is too

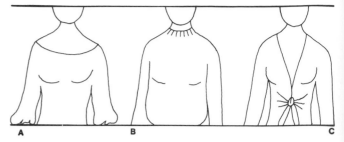

20 *If you have a full bust, you look good in these:*
A. Loose top of outfit and emphasis on lower part of the sleeves.
B. A larger-than-usual sweater.
C. Emphasis on cleavage.

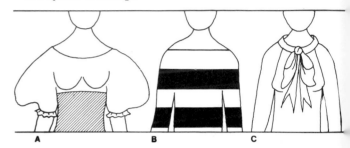

21 *If you have a full bust, you are not flattered by:*
A. Fussy upper sleeves and lighter upper outfit.
B. Horizontal stripes emphasizing bustline.
C. Ties falling over the bust.

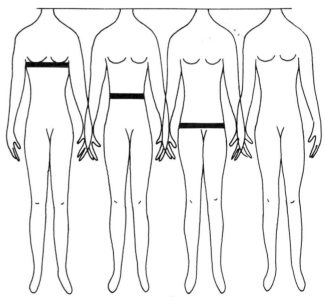

22 *Find your best 'dividing line'. Either nude or in a simple one-piece outfit, stand in front of a full-length mirror and tie a scarf or belt below the bust, round the waist and on the hips. Which looks best? Do you look better, perhaps, with no divider at all?*

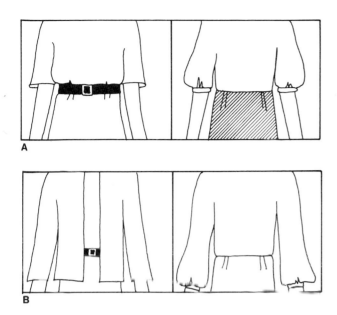

23 *If you have a wide waist:*
A. You should avoid obvious belts and a colour change at the waist.
B. You will look better in tops extending below the waist, and in no colour change at the waist.

tight, or a full skirt with prominent front zip or other fastening). You will look better in slightly looser skirts and belts, and try to have fastenings at the back.

If your *buttocks* are your problem, avoid bringing emphasis to them. You will feel happier in skirts and trousers that are not too tight; try to bring emphasis to the upper part of your body with softly falling jackets or sweaters that fall to the hips. If your buttocks are too large, go for darker-coloured skirts or trousers and A-line garments; if your buttocks are too small emphasize the waist with a prominent belt.

Height is also an important factor. If you are *tall* you will look good in horizontal bands (wide bands are more flattering than narrow stripes), hip divider, long necklace-type neckline with emphasis on shoulders, trousers (especially those of unusual length – many 'full length' trousers are too short, anyway, so capitalize on this deficiency). Tall people only emphasize their height when they wear vertical stripes, below-bust dividing lines, hemline just on the knee, fussy 'little girl' frills (and black stockings with a white dress!), a frumpy old-hippie skirt not full enough, or one main garment with no 'break' at the waist.

24 *If you are tall you look good in these:*
A. Horizontal bands.
B. Hip divider and long necklace-type neckline.
C. Emphasis on shoulders, trousers of unusual length.

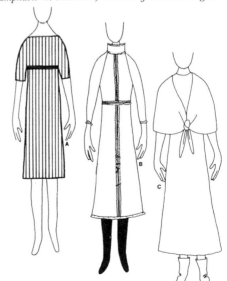

25 *Similarly, if you are tall you should avoid:*
A. Narrow vertical stripes, below-bust dividing line and hemline just on the knee.
B. Fussy 'little girl' frills (and black stockings with a white dress!)
C. Frumpy old-hippie skirt not full enough.

29

26 *If you are short, you look good in:*
A. Simple seaming.
B. One-piece loose-fitting trousers.
C. If you have a horizontal divider, it is better to have both sides the same colour.

27 *By the same token, if you are short you should avoid:*
A. Obvious horizontal stripes.
B. Fussy frills and hip emphasis (and, as here, lacy legs which bring the eye down).
C. Similarly, the eye is here brought down to the lower legs (and too-tight and layered clothes do not look good).

By the same tokens, if you are *short* you look good in simple seaming, diagonal lines which bring the beholder's eye upwards, unobtrusive hem lengths, one-piece outfits, loose-fitting trousers and simple vertical lines. Where there is a horizontal divider, it is better to have both sides the same colour and divert the eye elsewhere, preferably upwards.

(NB. Vary your hem lengths!) Short women will find that horizontal stripes exaggerate their lack of height, as do fussy frills, layered clothes, hip emphasis and lacy legs, which bring the eye down.

If you are *small* you should in the main simply follow the maxims for shorter people (above). If you are downright *big*, you must be careful what you wear, as in pale colours and lots of frills you may look like a doll in fancy dress.

(If you are tall, short, small, big or otherwise distinguished and if you have problems finding clothes, see 'Special People', chapter 7.)

So – be honest with yourself. Wear what *suits* you.

What do you need from your clothes?

Before you assess what you *think* you need from your clothes, discipline yourself to fill out this chart for a whole week. You can start any day, but try to complete the whole week.

At the end of the week, ask yourself:

(**a**) Were any clothes uncomfortable (e.g. skirts with too-tight waists)?

(**b**) Which of the clothes you wore do you consider good buys?

(**c**) Are there any obvious gaps in your wardrobe as it is at the moment?

All the 'guinea pigs' who filled out sample forms admitted that analysing one week's clothing had

	Mon	Tues	Wed	Thurs	Fri	Sat	Sun
	(example)						
getting up/ breakfast	robe						
during morning	jeans, blue T-shirt, tennis shoes						
lunch	pink shirtwaist dress, black shoes*						
afternoon	,,						
early evening	changed shoes (flat gold), same dress						
supper/ dinner	,,						

Day's comments: *wrong – need paler-coloured shoes

taught them something. Maggie Rose, a retailing executive, for instance, is always meticulously dressed both at work and elsewhere, but she nonetheless confessed that one shirt was uncomfortable as a buttonhole was fraying and the button kept coming undone. Her 'best items' were a drawstring dress that she had made herself, and a mini-skirt converted from a three-tiered skirt she had had when she was thirteen. She thought, on reflection, that she needed more, and better co-ordinating, accessories. Similarly, at the end of her week, Diana May thought she needed a lightweight rainproof jacket (which she has since bought!).

At the end of your week you should be able to work out more accurately what you actually wear. Obviously this is going to be determined not only by your shape but also by:

1 Your age
Nothing looks worse than a teenager in her grandmother's clothes and, by the same token, most grandmothers should show neither knees nor upper arms as a matter of course. Someone told me how one day she wore what she considered were some most attractive new shoes and her grandson looked at them seriously and said 'I know you are old, but there is no need to look as if you are.' (Special information for young and old is included in chapter 7.)

2 Where you live
Those who live in London, Hong Kong, New York or other high-fashion cities may need more pairs of high heels, for instance, than those who live in rural Dorset. And those who live in the colder parts of the world are certainly going to need clothes that keep them warm. (NB. If you work in New York you will also need the ubiquitous 'trainers' to walk to and from work. You either carry your main shoes or have them already in the office, and put them on when you get there!)

Jan Rae is an American journalist married to a Scot. They live in Edinburgh and she knows from experience how to beat Scottish draughts:

Scotland's chill breezes call for a certain amount of practical planning on the part of its fashion-conscious women. Knitwear, jackets, shawls and waistcoats are an important part of every wardrobe, since they can be used to top almost any outfit, adding a touch of glamour as well as warmth.

In addition to the traditional tweeds and knitwear (most Scottish women buy cottons chiefly for holidays abroad!) here are some useful items to protect you against the Scottish elements: 1. A raincoat; 2. a thermal vest to wear under silk blouses (and long-johns to wear under long skirts, if you are bound for a draughty castle); 3. a sheepskin or padded coat or bodywarmer; 4. High boots or warm trousers.

28 *Dress your age! (Jeunes Filles at British Home Stores).*

By comparison, Mackay Crampton lives in Malibu, California. Some evenings get quite chilly and I have had to wear a sweater when visiting her – but in the main, her year-round wardrobe consists of lightweight high fashion and 'relaxed elegance' clothes.

3 Whether you are home-based or working away from home

If you spend most days busy at home you may need only a pair of blue jeans and several sweaters. If, on the other hand, you are receptionist at a local hairdresser's and you are not given a uniform, you might need many different changes of chic clothes (see 'Work Clothes', chapter 9).

This is where the concept of the 'basic wardrobe' comes in.

Basic wardrobe

The concept of the basic wardrobe is that with the minimum number of clothes you will gain the maximum versatility for your particular needs. With the fewest possible clothes you save money, storage space and time. You know, now that you have read the previous chapter, what your particular needs are. Now you can determine your ideal basic wardrobe.

In Britain, for instance, most people need only three different 'groups' of clothes:

1 Winter.

2 Spring/autumn.

3 Holidays (worn occasionally, and also when summer comes!).

In North America, however, most people need three slightly different categories of clothes:

1 Winter.

2 Between-season.

3 Summer (including long-sleeved **gar**ments or sweaters to cope with intense air-**con**ditioning).

Here are some sample wardrobes in the three groups, for home-based and working women in Britain:

Sample wardrobes

1 Winter wardrobe for a home-based woman
(basic colours: brown, green, yellow)

	day	*evening*
coats	brown tweed cape green leather jacket	brown velvet jacket
skirts, etc.	full-length brown/green brown-green tweed green culottes jeans	paisley viyella
dresses	yellow-brown patterned two-piece	dark green jersey
blouses	selection, some wool	
sweaters	brown cardigan V-necked long-sleeved brown beige guernsey	

2 Spring through autumn wardrobe for a home-based woman
(basic colours: beige, green, navy, yellow)

	day	*evening*
coats	lightweight raincoat (brown velvet) (green leather)	
skirts, etc.	(jeans) beige A-line yellow-green pleated	(full-length viyella)
dresses	(yellow-brown patterned)	navy jersey plain
blouses	(as before) + some short-sleeved	
sweaters	beige cardigan (beige guernsey) navy cotton short-sleeved	

3 Basic holiday/summer wardrobe for a home-based woman
(basic colours: green, navy, pink, turquoise, yellow)

	day	*evening*
coats	(lightweight raincoat)	pink shawl
skirts, etc.	pink wrap-round white culottes white shorts	yellow-pink peasant
dresses	navy/yellow sundress short-sleeved green shift long-sleeved pink cotton	yellow 'blousey'
blouses	assorted	
sweaters	white cardigan	
plus	bikini swimsuit kanga	

4 Winter wardrobe for a working woman
(*basic colours: beige, black, red*)

	day	evening
coats	good trenchcoat with lining red leather blouson jacket	black shawl
suits	black Chanel-type (jacket can be worn by itself)	
skirts	2 daytime, to go with suit	1 long
dresses	red/black patterned beige	kaftan plain black
blouses	6 assorted	(at least 1 silk)
leisure	jeans cardigan assorted sweaters	

5 Spring/autumn wardrobe for a working woman
(*basic colours: beige, red, turquoise*)

	day	evening
coats	(trenchcoat) (red blouson)	(black shawl)
suits	(black Chanel) beige, with blazer jacket	
skirts, etc	2 daytime 1 short culottes	1 long culottes
dresses	turquoise striped beige/blue patterned red/beige patterned	(1 plain black) (kaftan)
blouses	(as before) + 1 sleeveless + 1 short-sleeved	
leisure	(as before) + lightweight cotton sweaters	

6 Holiday/summer wardrobe for a working woman
(*basic colours: beige, black, pink, turquoise, white*)

	day	evening
coats	(trenchcoat) (beige suit jacket)	(black shawl)
skirts, etc.	pink wrap-round beige culottes	white peasant long pink frilled
dresses	pink/white striped sundress short-sleeved turquoise shift long-sleeved white cotton	short 'blousey' black (kaftan)
blouses	selection	
leisure	(jeans) bikini swimsuit kanga	

Having read these sample basic wardrobes, why not try making your own? It need only take half an hour.

Good dressing is the result not simply of good luck but of good planning.

What you need to complement what you already have

It may be that you already own your ideal basic wardrobe. Most people, however, need at least several new purchases or 'makes' to satisfy their requirements.

Go to your wardrobe and drawers and take out *every* item. Make a checklist. Put to one side anything that:

(**a**) Does not match an item on your basic wardrobe list.

(**b**) Does not go with at least two other items.

(**c**) Has not been worn in the last nine months.

(**d**) Is completely wrong as far as colour is concerned (see 'Colour', chapter 4).

The items put to one side can be stored for future use or discarded (see below for ways of selling). Never be afraid to get rid of clothes.

29 *Versatile patterned two-piece dress (Londonpride Viyella).*

Ask those around you

You know what you should or should not wear, both for your lifestyle and for your shape. But *do* remember the maxim that you should not wear *anything* unless you are happy in it.

Often you will feel happiest in clothes that are pleasing to those around you. Try asking the man in your life what he enjoys seeing you in.

The husband of one of the best-dressed women in this book does not generally like women in hats or trousers, especially the baggy sort. He does not like clothes that are too clingy, tight or revealing: he prefers 'the hint of hidden promise'. He does like his wife's hair down.

30 Jocelyn Andrews, 6, would ideally like to see her mother in pale pistachio, white, pink and blue.

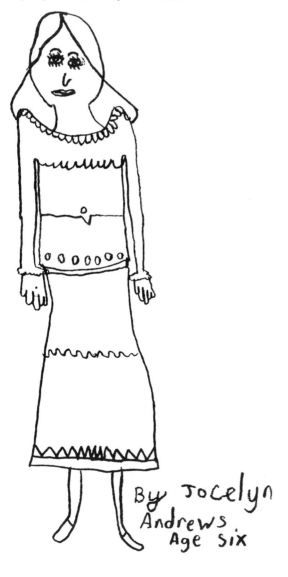

By Jocelyn Andrews. Age Six

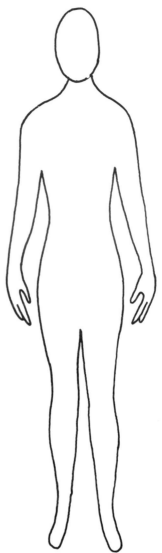

31 Why not ask your children to dress you in an appropriate manner?

Ask your children what *they* think about your clothes.

Jocelyn Andrews is 6. She does not like seeing her mother in trousers ('because they do not look good on her'). Jocelyn does not notice accessories much, but she does not like hats. Ideally, she would like to see her mother wearing a pale pistachio-coloured dress embellished with pale-pink embroidery and added frills, and with blue-and-white buttons.

Well, that is what Jocelyn would like. Here is a basic figure . . . why not ask those around you what they would like to draw on it for you to wear?

CHAPTER 4

Colour

What is colour?

Colour in dressing is putting together a palette that complements you. What colours those should be depends on:

1 Your own colouring.

2 Your mood.

3 Your environment.

I went to San Antonio, Texas, to talk to a leading colour specialist, Wilanna Bristow, and as we sat over margaritas and tortillas we talked about colour.

> People always look better in colours that do something for them. There is a personal relationship in how colour is used on an individual basis, and much of it people are not aware of at all, on a conscious level. They perceive colour on a subliminal level and their colour information grows through the years, and depending on depression, on the horror they have understood and their joys, all this will have a bearing on how they personally feel about colour.
>
> Environment and personal influences all have bearing on colour. I personally have adopted a lot of Mexican colour sense by living so near the Mexican border. In a depressed economy people use colour to brighten up their lives.
>
> Colour can have negative or positive qualities. Blue, for instance, is the colour frequently associated with depression – and sometimes with obesity and sweetness, sugar (blue, for instance, is a good colour for packaging sugar!). On the positive side, however, blue is associated with stability and that is why successful business people often wear blue suits.
>
> Black and white can express sophistication, because they are diametrically opposite to each other.

Pastel colours are normally considered feminine, particularly in chiffon or silk. But think of Hana Morae clothes: her bright clothes look much more feminine on a black woman than a white woman.

A lot of colour is established several years ahead. Those people who are in the know are going to make sure they are aware of the coming colours.

How much colour?

You will notice that the suggested basic wardrobes in this book all revolve around three colours. The concept of such a trio requires that:

1 All three go together.

2 At least one is a 'hub' colour (black, brown, navy, grey, beige, white).

Red, black and beige will therefore fit these requirements. Red, yellow and pink will not.

The point of a hub colour is to unite items. It may cover everyday accessories, say black shoes and bag. It will probably be the colour of some of the main clothing, say a coat. A winter hub colour can carry through to spring/autumn in the form of a black fabric bag, but a summer hub such as white shoes cannot be taken into winter.

Highlight colours complement the chosen basics. With the 'red, black and beige' wardrobe a highlight of turquoise – say shoes and skirt – can look stunning with at least two of the chosen basics (black and beige). A wardrobe without highlight colours is boring; so is a monochromatic wardrobe.

Highlights provide versatility, an essential ingredient of successful dressing. Colours reflect an image, and it is a good idea not always to present the *same* image. Yellows, for instance, are vivacious and bright, whereas blues suggest coolness and calm. Purples indicate a bold superiority and reds are aggressively exciting.

Give some thought to that versatility. Get some coloured pencils or markers and try different colour ways on these sketches: what effects do the colour combinations have?

32, 33, 34 *These are sketches by Manila designer Backie Celdran: why not try colouring them in different colourways?*

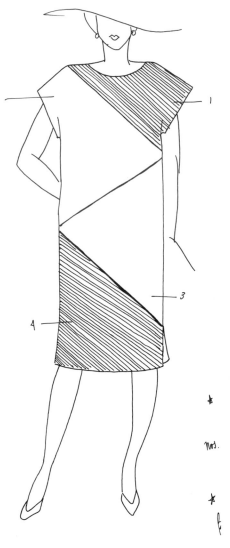

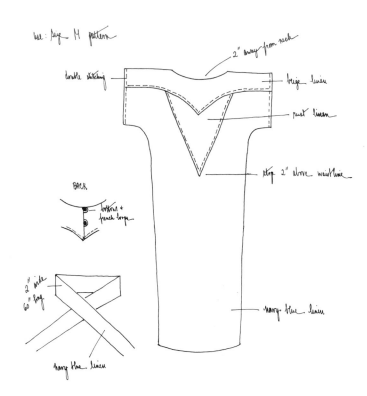

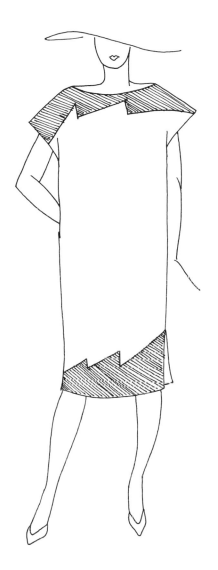

Learn about colour

I asked Wilanna Bristow how can you start to learn about colour and she said, immediately, 'be curious'.

'Knowing the general vanity of most women – and I say this in the kindest way – they will be curious about what colours do the best for them, and I think that people who are selling colour capitalize on this.'

Your mood

Clarita Seibold is from El Salvador and has lived all over the world with her husband, an international top hotelier. Clarita has an extensive wardrobe ('doesn't every woman love clothes?' she said laughingly when we talked in Caracas, Venezuela).

She was wearing bright royal blue for a formal dinner she gave in my honour, and her long chestnut hair was knotted up into an Edwardian loose upper 'bun'. Clarita says she wears pink if she needs to bolster her feelings. A few days later, when we had a relaxed lunch *a deux*, she was casually wearing ecru colour-matched blouse and skirt which superbly complemented her glorious hair, now down.

Try jotting down, over the space of a week, the colours you have worn each day. Each night, before you go to bed, also frankly admit your feelings that day:

See how colours you put on first thing in the morning might have reflected what you anticipated the day would bring. Observe, too, that if you felt, for instance, anger during the day, you may have changed into a relaxing pale blue outfit at night, as if to compensate.

Incidentally, we probably all see colours slightly differently. Calma Kohler, for instance, found that after her corneal graft she could close one eye and see a colour as tending to purple, then she could close the other and see the same item as tending to blue . . .

	Mon	Tues	Wed	Thurs	Fri	Sat	Sun
main colours worn							
what feelings did I have today (e.g.was I angry? confident? happy?)							

We therefore probably all associate the same colour with differing emotions. Here are some of the emotions that occur to me:

Black – defiant, confident

White – contentment, determination to be artistic

Navy blue – traditional, reserved, quietly confident

Pale blue – reserved satisfaction

Yellow, orange – liable to anger

Red – undiverted confidence

Why not take a moment to jot down, here, what you associate with various colours? (This makes rather a good party game!)

	emotional association
black	
browns	
blues	
greens	
oranges	
purples	
reds	
yellows	
whites	

Your environment

I started writing this chapter while researching in Hawaii. Here is what I was wearing at the time: lime green dress with red/white/blue/green art nouveau necklace and matching earrings, gardenia in my hair and blue nail varnish . . .

Enough said. If I wore the same clothes at home in England I would be thought to be decidedly – rather than mildly – bohemian.

Remember that it is not only fabric type that requires suitable environments (e.g. tweeds in Scotland), but also the colour of those fabrics

and their accessories. Electric colours require sun. Soft muted colours, by contrast, would look terrible in Hawaii but marvellous in the Hebrides.

Help with colour

Colour co-ordinating companies help you to look your best with minimal effort.

Colour Me Beautiful, started by Carole Jackson, is the best-known international company, with available services throughout North America, Japan, Britain and Europe and South Africa. There are nearly 400 consultants (including some men) worldwide.

Mary Spillane, Managing Director for Colour Me Beautiful for Britain and Europe, says:

> We are a service industry, giving the woman power to make the most of herself. Colour is the first step in getting your look together. Next the programme goes into clothing styles and assessment, make-up and wardrobe planning. Our goal is to help women enhance their *own* natural beauty and to give them confidence in their image.

A typical colour analysis with one of Colour Me Beautiful's highly trained consultants lasts about three hours. Ideally, five or six clients take part at once, to encourage inter-action and ideas. This costs less than, say, a skirt which you could have bought as a 'mistake' if you did not know which colours suit you best. You are given a small wallet with your 'best' colour swatches and the idea is that you carry this with you in your handbag whenever you are shopping. The follow-up classes are for half or full-day sessions.

I had lunch with Pamela Schaecher, a former interior decorator who heads Colour Me Beautiful for Belgium, Luxembourg and the Netherlands. She feels strongly that colour analysis is ideal for both young people and older people 'who lose hair and skin tones so that what they wear is all the more important: I had one client not long ago who telephoned me the other day to say her husband says she now looks five years younger wearing her "correct" colours!'

CHAPTER 5

Materials

This chapter is all about some *special materials* – properties of many others are given in the 'Clothes care' chapter (16).

Batik

Printed textiles looking like batik are now readily available and, individual and beautiful though they are, you might wonder at the high cost of buying real batik, which has been resist-dyed using wax to cover parts of the fabric not to be given a particular colour.

The best batiks come from the Indonesian island of Java. If you are lucky enough to go there, you can actually see the process in all its stages, with men and women working in large airy open-sided sheds, babies swinging in batik hammocks and hens clucking.

First, 100% cotton is washed and then a design is drawn in pencil. Areas not to be coloured by the first dye are either stamped, with a shaped iron dipped in wax, or drawn with a bamboo pen, called a canting, which 'writes' with melted wax. The required pattern must be marked twice on the fabric: right way round on one side and mirror image on the reverse.

The first dyeing gives the cloth its background colour, which is usually dark blue or brown. The wax is removed, and a second colour is added by a similar method.

After all the colours have been dyed and all wax removed, the fabric is soaked in a solution of lime and water to help fix the dyes and improve their sheen. Many think that batik becomes increasingly beautiful with age, and cotton batik should wash well, although it is a good idea to wash it separately from other items, especially at first.

The batik process is now also being applied to chiffon and other silks. (Some of the furnishing fabric batiks are also outstanding.)

Beads

Beading made-up garments is difficult, as the fabric has to be stretched on a frame before it can be worked on. Much beading is done with a tambour hook, rather like a crochet hook, which produces a continuous chain, with each link over the radius of a different bead.

35 *Gorgeous hand-beaded jacket based on the traditional phoenix and dragon 'qua' worn by Chinese brides (jacket by Jenny Lewis, photograph by Kevin Orpin, courtesy Hong Kong Trade Development Council)*

Cashmere

Cashmere is soft but warm and light to wear — the yarn comes from combings from under the fleece of Cashmere goats from the high altitude areas of China and Mongolia.

Unlike wool, cashmere is painstakingly hand-combed rather than sheared, and this is done annually, in spring. Only the soft under-hair closest to the goat's skin is fine enough to be used, and it takes the under-hair of 24 goats to make an overcoat.

Most cashmere combings are brought, matted and oily, to Scotland: Dawson International are the world's largest cashmere processors (they are the parent company of Pringle of Scotland, Braemar and many other well-known names). The combings are scoured and cleaned, and about half is generally considered of sufficient quality to become Scottish cashmere. After dyeing, fibres are teased out so that they lie roughly in the same direction and oil is added to give resilience during carding and spinning. The oil is later removed.

Cotton

Cotton is easy to wear, and adaptable. Worn as a loose garment, it can be cool: when knitted or worn as layers it can entrap warmth.

I find that, for instance, a black cotton dress with long sleeves can be worn more or less anywhere and in most climates. It really is amazingly versatile.

The International Institute for Cotton says that one of cotton's greatest virtues is that it is easy and safe to wash. They recommend frequent washing before articles become really dirty, and point out that it is important only to use the specified amount of powder or detergent. Most household whites can be boiled, and even bleached, to remove stains.

Fur

Diana May says:

> Try not to wear your fur every day. It will be better if rested from time to time. If it is long-haired, use a wide-tooth comb very gently on it, using light pressure just on the surface to comb the hairs against the fall of the pile – that is, if the pile falls downwards brush the hairs with an upwards movement. With a close-pile fur like Persian lamb, use a very soft hairbrush to run across the surface. If

your fur becomes damp, shake out and then hang it in a cool dry place with freshly circulating air – *never* dry close to a fire or a radiator. Always hang your fur on a well-padded hanger with lots of space around it, preferably covered with a cotton or silk cover (not plastic, which encourages condensation).

Here are some other tips for looking after your fur:

1 Friction caused by seat belts and synthetic upholstery when in a car can make a fur look 'worn'. If possible, take your coat off when you are driving.

2 Hair spray and perfume can dry out natural oils and make the skin brittle.

3 Worn with a fur coat, shoulder bags can damage the shoulder areas.

Leather

The term 'leather' denotes an animal skin, not its surface finish. It includes both grain (what is often simply called 'leather') and suede.

Grain leather is finished on the outside (i.e. the hair or wool side of the skin).

Suede leather is obtained by several methods:

(**a**) The grain surface of any leather may be buffed to reveal a finer suede nap.

(**b**) The grain surface may be split off to reveal a suede surface (this is known as 'suede split').

(**c**) The underside of the skin may be used.

Buying

Buy the best quality that you can afford. A little extra financial sacrifice will return dividends in giving you longer wear, smartness and greater enjoyment. Only buy branded garments into which a label is sewn, and always buy from a shop that specializes in leather. Ask the salesperson what kind of skin has been used and ask advice in how to look after your garment.

It is difficult to do your own 'performance tests' in a shop, but if you touch an unseen corner of the garment with a wet handkerchief you can see how it absorbs moisture – this is a good indication of its rainproof qualities. Similarly, rubbing a piece of suede both inside and outside a garment with a white handkerchief is a reasonable indicator of the amount of colour that may come off later.

36 *Leather extravaganza – two-piece outfit by Chris Brad-bury with silver cape leather and coloured beads (courtesy Pittards).*

Wear and tear

Be careful when wearing your leather coat on 'flag' days: do not let any charity sellers stick an adhesive label on your coat as it discolours the skin and the mark cannot always be removed by dry cleaning.

Leathers can be cleaned at home by wiping the surface with a damp – not soaking – sponge and diluted solution of liquid detergent (1 part to 5 parts of water).

The safest method of home care for suede and sheepskins is gently to brush the pile up and down after approximately one month's wear, and regularly thereafter. If grease should get on the garment, brush a little talcum powder over the affected area, leave it for an hour or so and lightly brush away. The talc may absorb some of the grease and also lighten the mark.

Take your leather, suede or sheepskin coat to be cleaned at a reputable shop regularly – and certainly before heavy soiling sets in. Go to a company that specializes in the care of leathers.

Pittards are one of the main British leather producers: they tan and dye the skins that companies make into shoes, coats and other garments. Pittards sell skins direct to the public only at their regular twice-yearly Saturday sales.

Linen

Remember the era when you – or your mother or grandmother – automatically went into a 'uniform' of dark blue linen suit the moment summer arrived? It creased terribly . . .

Now that same creasing is being used to dramatic effect by such designers as Thomas Wee (see chapter 12, Around the world). He deliberately creates unlined linen co-ordinates in stunning bright colours (apple green, dark buttercup yellow, royal blue). You 'mix and match' and the creases intentionally add to the relaxed effect of the garments.

Silk

Threads of the cocoon of the Bombyx mori moth are unreeled to produce a continuous filament up to 1,000 metres long. The various stages in looking after the moths and preparation of the threads and subsequent weaving into fabric are now to some extent mechanized, and silk garments are increasingly being worn even for everyday purposes – thanks to a large extent to the efforts of the European Commission for the Promotion of Silk who produce excellent informative leaflets on silk and how to look after it.

Silk was discovered around 2600BC in China – according to one legend, the Empress Si-Ling-Chi accidentally dropped a cocoon into a cup of hot liquid, which melted the gum holding the cocoon together so that it unravelled into two continuous fibres. Sericulture, the cultivation of silkworms for silk, spread both to Japan and India and by the fifth century production had reached Europe.

Emma Woodman works for Royal Silk, the world's largest mail-order silk shirt company. She says:

Silk is the strongest of all natural fibres. Unbelievably, a thread of silk is stronger than steel of the same diameter. Its strength is due to the fact that silk is the only fibre which occurs in a continuous filament, with a usable length of up to 3,000 feet. Silk is a highly absorbent fabric. It can hold 11%

37 *One of the most useful ingredients of many wardrobes —
a plain silk shirt (courtesy Royal Silk).*

38 *Janice Wainwright dress using a silk satin fabric with gold metallic stripes by Clerici Tessuto (hair by Trevor at Colombe of Motcomb Street, shoes by Charles Jourdan, photograph by Roger Eaton, courtesy European Commission for the Promotion of Silk).*

of its weight in water (compared to 8% for cotton and only 4% for nylon). This makes silk ideal for summer wear. It is a poor conductor of heat and is therefore surprisingly warm in winter. It generates very little static, and it is both resilient and elastic.

Here are some of the silks you may come across:

Habutai – Japanese broadcloth, wears and launders well.

Fuji – lightweight fabric made from short silk fibres from the ends of cocoons, usually made into shirts and blouses.

Pongee – textured fabric, woven with a mixture of thick and thin wild silk fibres (see Tussah).

Raw – silk that has not undergone the usual degumming process.

Shantung – slightly irregularly-surfaced plain-weave wild silk (see Tussah).

39, 40, 41 *In Hong Kong, silk arrives in bales from China: after being spun and woven, it is hand-printed (still very much a manly skill); women work hard to make up orders (photographed in Hong Kong, courtesy Cathay Pacific).*

Tussah – wild silk from the cocoon of Tussah silkworm which lives on oak leaves (as opposed to mulberry leaves). The tannin in the oak leaves gives wild silk a distinct tan colour. The fabric has a coarse, textured surface and is durable and washable.

Wear and tear

The European Commission for the Promotion of Silk recommends that silk ties and scarves should always be dry-cleaned – as should any other item, unless the manufacturer specifically says it can be carefully hand-washed, say in Woolite.

It is always worth doing a simple 'dye test' before washing. Wet a small corner of the item in cool water and place it on a piece of white fabric, press with a warm iron and see if any colour is removed.

If no colour runs, wash carefully by hand in lukewarm water with a gentle liquid detergent such as Woolite. Rinse well, in cold water, roll in a towel to squeeze out surplus moisture and dry away from the sun or direct heat. When it is still slightly damp, iron on the wrong side with a warm iron.

Spots and stains

The Royal Silk Company recommends acting quickly. If the silk is washable (see above), rinse immediately in lukewarm or cold water.

Deodorant stains can be removed by rinsing in cold water, then sponging on a solution of equal parts ammonia and water.

Grease spots can be removed with white tailor's chalk or white talcum powder. Sprinkle a little powder on the stain, put blotting paper above and beneath the fabric and iron the stain through the blotter.

Perspiration stains can be removed with white vinegar.

Water stains will be removed next time you wash the garment or have it cleaned.

Viyella

Viyella, a mixture of 55% merino wool and 45% cotton, was first registered in 1894. It is named after the Via Gellia Mill near Matlock, Derbyshire, owned by Henry Hollins who commissioned a yarn that would retain the best qualities of both wool and cotton while remaining strong enough to withstand the rigours of machine weaving.

Today William Hollins is part of the Vantona Viyella Group who produce Viyella Pure Wool and a 100% wool Challis as well as the basic viyella fabric. There are also ready-made collections for women: Londonpride – a collection of classic separates; and Viyella Limited Edition (classic clothes, sleek 100% wool flannel jackets, trousers and skirts co-ordinating with viyella shirts and knitwear in a variety of yarns).

Wool

'The home of quality wool fabrics is traditionally Britain', Chairman of the British Fashion Council, Cyril Kern, says. 'Tartans, cashmere, tweeds, lambswool and so on . . . fashion is taken from the traditional British style and evolved by the French, giving the 'Gallic Touch', the Italians' 'Latin touch' and the USA 'Americanization'. Fashion trends evolve by moving around the world.'

Wool fibre lengths vary from 4 to 40cm, and the best wool comes from the sheep's shoulders. It is extremely resilient and absorbent.

Types of wool fabric

Barathea – twill weave, made from worsted yarns. It has a smooth surface and is springy to handle.

Bouclé – woven in looped, knobbly yarns.

Challis – fine, plain-weave lightweight fabric.

Crêpe – twisted yarns can form different weights of springy fabric which frays easily.

Flannel – lightweight, soft, warm and resilient wool or worsted which does not easily fray.

Gaberdine – close twill weave, very springy fabric.

Melton – medium weight, plain weave fabric, sometimes slightly felted.

Mousseline – lightweight plain or printed fabric.

Tweed – hard-wearing strong, warm fabric with a heavy weave.

Woollen cloths vary wonderfully in texture and feel; garments drape and move beautifully and 'feel good'. Wool knitwear is soft and long-lasting (see Sweaters section in chapter 6).

(Similar to wool in some respects are angora, the long smooth fibres from the angora rabbit, and mohair, formed of fibres from the mohair goat and often woven into medium to heavyweight hairy fabric for jackets and coats. Care and attention for both should be as for wool.)

42 *Viyella's house check (navy, stone and red) was specially designed to celebrate the company's 200th anniversary in 1984 (photograph courtesy Viyella Limited Edition).*

CHAPTER 6

Underwear and accessories

Underwear

As with accessories, underwear can make or mar an outfit. Nothing looks worse than bulges around a badly-fitting bra showing through an outfit (especially if dirty bra straps are also revealed), and little can equal in repellence the outlines of underpants visible through trousers.

Some people, especially slim people with standard figures, will feel there is little point in investing in anything but chain-store bras, underpants and slips. If you do find a style that suits and fits you, buy in bulk, as styles change, and sometimes front-opening bras, for instance, do not seem to be available in winter.

To avoid having bra-straps showing, attach small tapes to the inside of shoulder seams of garments. The tapes are sewn on at the neck end, with Velcro (touch-and-close fastener) spots at the other.

43, 44 *You need the right bra for the right outfit (sketches courtesy Playtex).*

Bras
by Gillian Hutcheon

A woman needs a 'good foundation', first to make her feel good . . . if she feels good, ten to one she will look good too! A woman's underwear makes up the foundation of an overall appearance, whether it be sophisticated, sporty or just plain pretty. What you need is a combination of quality, style and value for money. You also need the right bra for you, and for your outfit.

A surprising number of women – 75%, estimates Playtex – walk around in a bra that does not fit correctly.

Buying bras

You can avoid a poor fit if you take the time to: (*a*) Determine (not guess) your bra size before you shop; and (*b*) try on a bra before you buy it.

1 To size yourself up, first wrap a tape measure around your body, directly under the breasts. Do this bra-less. Add 12cm (5in.) to this number to get your under-bust size. Next, measure your cup size. Wearing a bra, measure around the widest part of your bust (it is usually right on line with your nipples). If that number is 2.5cm (1in.) larger than your under-bust measurement, you wear an A cup; if 5cm (2in.) larger, a B cup; 7.5cm (3in.) larger, a C cup; 10cm (4in.) larger, a D cup.

2 Playtex suggest that to get a better-fitting bra, women should apply the following checklist:

(*a*) Bra edges should lie flat. Bulges mean cups are too small. Check under arms: an overhang means cups or band may be too small.

(*b*) Bra centre: check the junction of bra and breast bone. A bra should touch – but not poke – the body.

(*c*) Bra band: slip two fingers under the band in front. Too tight? Go up a size. Raise both arms overhead. Check rear view – if band rides up in the back, it is too big and breasts will hang down, unsupported. The correct band position is under the shoulder blades.

(*d*) Bra straps smooth out cups but should not support the breasts. Support comes from the cups and sides. To test, drop a strap off one shoulder. If that breast drops, the bra is not giving you support.

(*e*) Bra and clothes: put on a sweater and check that the bra shapes you in a way you like. Does anything show that you wish did not?

Bra styles

It may be that if a bra does not fit it is not the size but the style that is wrong. Here is a rundown of style options:

A *soft-cup bra* has a seamless cup made of stretchy material. It smooths you but will not give much support for larger sizes.

A *lightly-padded bra* gives a shape and definition without adding inches. This is good for in-between cup sizes.

45 *Soft-cup bra with special waist fastening so that you can wear it under a backless dress (Whispers by Playtex).*

An *under-wired bra* is good for medium to large, soft or pendulous breasts. It gives lift, support and separation – cleavage.

The cups on a *demi-bra* are cut a bit lower and often have a bit of contouring in the bottom of the cup to lift, support and enhance an average bosom.

A *minimizer bra* can trim 1–2½ inches off your bustline without making you look flattened.

Looking after your bras
Check washing instructions on the label of the garment (Playtex bras, for instance, always have clearly labelled instructions). If you have any complaints, contact the Customer Service Bureau at the national headquarters of the manufacturer concerned.

From a hygiene point of view, why not make or buy a pretty lace bag, with zip? Every night, before going to bed, you can automatically drop your day's 'smalls' into it. When you next do a wash the whole thing, bag and all, goes into the washer and drier. With this method bra straps do not become irrevocably intertwined.

Girdles and corselettes
As with bras, it is best to check that your girdle or

corselette fits correctly. It should feel snug, without binding. It should control but, at the same time, allow you to breathe easily and comfortably. Make sure that when you sit down the girdle is long enough still to control your figure without producing bulges or rolls of flesh.

Underpants
I am afraid I have always found bodystockings, camiknickers and teddies extremely impractical. After going to the bathroom you have somehow to re-popper the under-crotch connector. I once tried replacing the poppers with Velcro (touch-and-close fastening) but the sticky strips of fastening kept on getting caught on my tights (pantihose).

French knickers are comfortable to wear and do not 'show' when you are wearing trousers. They are perhaps the most elegant – and sexy – of all underpants.

The most sensible twentieth-century underpants I have ever come across look like men's G-strings: there is a broad elastic waistband from which hangs a crotch-coverer that is narrow in front and broad at the back. The pants are really comfortable to wear – and nothing 'shows' under trousers or cut-away leotards.

As with bras, do change your underpants regularly. There is a growing trend today, in-

46 *Underwired bra to give a good cleavage (Body Language by Playtex).*

50

deed, for wearing sanitary trouser-liners at all times of the month. (Particularly when you are staying in a hotel, it can be embarrassing to have to hand over dirty underpants to a laundry valet: a good tip is either to soak the whole garment or at least the offending area and hand over a wet – but clean – item!)

Nightwear

There is such pretty nightwear around today – but many still stick traditionally to a man's nightshirt or their own preferred garments.

Unlike daytime undergarments, nightwear does not have to fit. When buying, you should concentrate on quality, as sometimes less expensive items are made of fabric that can scratch. Do think, too, about who will see what you wear. If you are likely to stay with friends or in a hotel, don't choose anything too diaphanous!

Accessories

Accessories can make or mar an outfit – and the only important maxim is not to overdo them. Another good rule to bear in mind with all accessories is that they should either be expensive and classic or inexpensive and fun.

Bags

Following the above rule, you can either invest in good bags that indicate how much money you have spent on them, or you can purchase bags that merely serve a practical purpose.

After years of travelling around and observing dressing around the world I am bold enough to suggest that you do *not* try to combine 'expensive look with minimum cost'. In Wing On street in Hong Kong, for instance, you can buy spurious 'designer-look' bags for a few dollars. They might look all right on the open street stall, but when you see them away from there it is immediately noticeable that the 'leather trim' is cheap plastic and that the 'identification logo' is an implausible substitute.

If you do not want to pay a lot for a good bag, buy a less expensive one that has no pretence. In the past plastic looked cheap. Today vinyl and

47 *Girdles and corselettes offer full support and a good fit: they need not be 'old fashioned' (photographs courtesy Playtex).*

other man-made materials are used to produce bags that are inexpensive and remarkably strong. Some of the best-value bags I have ever had have been brightly coloured 'shoulder sacks' from chain stores.

It really is worth going either for shoulder bags or handle-less 'envelopes' or 'wallets'. The former are useful at all times, say if you are shopping with two children in a push chair, or if you are trying to cope with luggage, tickets and potential handbag-snatchers while travelling. It is also useful to have your bag over your shoulder in the evening so that you have your hands free for managing glasses and buffet food, or merely for shaking hands. In the main, the old-fashioned wrist or hand-held squat bag with one or two short handles looks terribly dated today. If you carry a bag like this you will look older, regardless of your age.

So, having decided what kind of price and styles you want, how many bags do you need?

Anna Pearson is always stunningly and elegantly dressed. Her maxim with bags is that it is very dangerous to keep changing bags, as you tend to leave credit cards and other 'essentials' in the bag you have just left at home. At the moment she has two daytime bags, both Gucci – a black leather bag for winter and a navy fabric with leather trim for summer.

What about evening bags? Anna Pearson is an internationally known needlepoint (canvaswork) designer and teacher. Her evening-bag project consists of a suede bag with removable panel so that you can quickly insert a suitably-coloured needlepoint design or plain fabric to match your outfit.

My own favourite evening bag is a black woven straw bag from Cora Jacobs in Manila. Its only embellishment is a gigantic shell – which matches the decoration on a simple tie belt.

Belts

Generally, when you buy a dress with its own belt, it is the belt which may give away the fact that it was an inexpensive purchase. Change the belt, and the dress can look twice what you paid for it!

Even if you are not proud of your waist, a simple belt will make your outfit look more expensive (although if your waist really is globe-round, do not go for an obvious and outrageous belt – keep it simple).

A 'basic belt wardrobe' could consist of:

48 *Do not overdo accessories!*
A. Too many 'itsy bitsy' addenda.
B. By contrast, one more definite accessory complements a basic outfit.

(**a**) A thick black leather belt with simple gold or black buckle.

(**b**) A golden metal chain belt.

Keep leather belts either hanging up in your wardrobe or on a hook, or loosely rolled, right side out.

Glasses

The old adage that 'men don't make passes at girls who wear glasses' does not apply today. The range of available styles – from 'Dame Edna fly-aways' to 'granny specs' to barely-visible frames – means that you can choose glasses that really complement the shape of your face.

Glasses should also go with your activities. You might feel out of place wearing pale pink but-

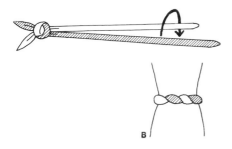

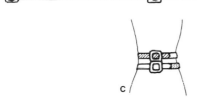

49 *Belt ideas:*
A. Wrap a scarf around your waist and put a belt on top.
B. If your dress has its own loose-tie belt, vary the look with a 'twist': knot the belt with a long scarf and twist the longer length round and round before knotting the other end (the twist belt can be worn with the ends in front or behind).
C. Take two ordinary buckled belts, say of contrasting colours, and make a double-belt, with the crossover of belts at the back.

50 *Fashion glasses suitably complementing the well-dressed woman (Cosmet 225 glasses by Neostyle).*

terfly frames with diamante stars when going to a parent–teacher meeting. Choose glasses that suit your face – and also your life.

When you try on a pair of glasses, check the frame from different angles. Ask to borrow a hand mirror (or take a compact with mirror) so that you can see what a particular style does for you side view on. Ask someone honestly what you look like.

If you really have bad eyesight, choosing a new pair of frames is particularly difficult, as you cannot see how you look. Then you do have to ask someone else's advice!

Gloves

Do you ever really need gloves from an etiquette point of view? Until just a few years ago I sometimes used to carry gloves (never wear them – they never fitted over my rings) when talking to ladies' clubs in different parts of the world. Now I find I travel with one pair of black leather gloves in case I need them for warmth in a cold country.

If you need gloves for warmth, a good basic wardrobe could include a pair of everyday wool gloves or mittens, and a pair of leather above-wrist gloves for more formal occasions.

Hats

Phoenix-like, hats have now become fashion accessories once again. For some years, many people had, say, one hat, which 'did' weddings and was borrowed by all and sundry for similar occasions.

Now, following the lead of the Princess of Wales and Princess Michael of Kent in Britain, it is *fun* to wear hats.

51, 52 If you want to get ahead, get a hat ... (photographs courtesy David Shilling and Revlon).

Many of the chain stores have good inexpensive hats, and you can sometimes add your own trimmings.

If you want a unique hat you need to go to a milliner like David Shilling – who first made his name with the gigantic head coverings worn annually by his mother at Ascot. Now David has a shop in Chiltern Street in London. He has made hats for bridesmaids of 18 months old, and one of his many well-known customers is a hat-loving nonogenarian.

David Shilling believes that a woman should present a balanced silhouette. It is not necessarily important whether you are tall and skinny or short and fat. The overall shape-picture presented by you, your outfit, your shoes and your hat is the vital point.

He prefers people to show him the dress or coat they will be wearing so that he knows what will complement his hat. If someone wants one of his hats with, say, the brim narrowed he will seldom do it, as this alters the whole balance of the hat's shape, but if they want it in a different colour that will usually be done. Colour must co-ordinate with the rest of the outfit but not necessarily match.

David Shilling finds that nature gives him the ideas for some of his designs. An outrageous swoop of gigantic petals formed of painted canvas, wrapped around the head as a medieval coif about to 'take off', for instance (how else would *you* describe figure 52?), derived inspiration from a Venetian sunset.

How on earth do you look after such a hat? No problem, says David. 'If one of my hats gets wet, for instance, I can always put it back on its original block (mould) and reshape it.'

David Shilling says many of his customers always hand-carry their hatboxes when they travel overseas. He suggests asking the flight attendants' help – nicely – they may even be amused.

Hats should, ideally, always be kept wrapped in acid-free tissue paper in special hatboxes, which are now sometimes difficult to find. If you have not got a lovely old box inherited from your grandmother, look out for a suitably-sized cardboard box at your supermarket checkout. Cover the outside with pretty wrapping paper, and if the box does not have a lid cut another piece of paper-covered card to fit. Remember to wrap the hat in acid-free tissue paper before putting it in its box.

Jewellery

Gold is measured in carats – pure gold is 24 carat, but this is so soft that it is rarely used. Gold is usually mixed with other metals to make alloys.

All jewellery containing any amount of real gold must be hallmarked by an Assay Office. Each hallmarked piece bears the following identifying symbols:

(**a**) Sponsor's mark (who made the piece)

(**b**) Quality mark (a crown, to show the piece is real gold)

(**c**) Standard mark (750 means it is 18 carat gold, 375 that it is 9 carat)

(**d**) Assay Office mark (a tiger's head shows that the piece was hallmarked by the London Assay Office)

(**e**) Year symbol.

(You can get information on gold from the Gold Information Bureau.)

Some stunning pieces of modern jewellery are being produced. The Hallmarking Act 1973 has strict provisions laid down about the use of base metals in precious jewellery, but in 1983 Edinburgh jeweller Graham Crimmins became the first artist to have a piece of mixed metal work (a titanium and silver ring) hallmarked.

For travelling, remember to leave your real jewellery at home or in the bank and resign yourself to make do with imitation. It is not worth risking the loss of your treasures, and in any case this arrangement provides a chance to try some of the exciting modern costume items available. Some of my favourites are brightly coloured plastic necklaces looking like lengths of coiled telephone wire, and dangly plastic earrings reminiscent of Christmas tree decorations!

Shoes

Julian Morgan is an Ambassador's wife. Since she is often overseas for many months at a time and cannot get regularly to her chosen shoe shops, she always buy two pairs of a favourite style at once.

How I wish I were disciplined enough to follow her advice . . . but invariably I find that by the time a pair of invaluable black leather pumps has worn out, the manufacturer has changed the style . . . (On the other hand, of

53 *The best-dressed woman never forgets her jewellery! (photograph courtesy British Home Stores).*

course, if you buy two pairs of shoes that do not turn out as well as expected, you have made a double mistake.)

Many people do not enjoy shopping for shoes. The whole exercise can be traumatic. Further difficulty is presented by the fact that there may be several shoe shops in the main shopping street. Some of these are owned by the same firm and have more or less the same shoes, but they are displayed differently enough to warrant inspection of each shop.

Perhaps the first thing to establish is how many pairs of shoes you need. Haphazardly buying shoes without ample forethought can result in a shoe wardrobe of three pairs of navy heels and a pair of gold slippers and nothing else.

54 Two practical winter designs with oriental flavour: the shoes, with low scooped heel, have two-tone lattice-work uppers, and the 'paddy boots' have heavy unit track soles and ruched legs in suede with leather piping (courtesy Russell & Bromley).

55 *Summer sandals are most practical if they have ankle ties or straps so that you can walk more easily – and no between-* *toe thongs make it possible, if necessary, to wear tights or socks (courtesy Russell & Bromley).*

Mary Bentham, Press Officer for Russell and
Bromley, limits her own shoe colouring to two
basics, black and taupe (or brown). She needs:

(most of the year):

(a) Black high- and low-heeled shoes.

(b) Taupe high- and low-heeled shoes.

(The black high-heeled shoes are worn in the
evening, and she does not own a pair of slippers –
she is a sock addict.)

(winter)

Two pairs of boots (she confesses to needing a
pair of wellingtons, too, but cannot bring herself
to buy even a pair of fashion wellies).

(summer)

(a) White low-heeled sandals.

(b) Black low-heeled sandals.

(c) Neutral (or taupe) low-heeled open-toed
pumps.

Question yourself. If you had to limit yourself to
five pairs of footwear (to cope with indoors and
out, and all temperatures) what would you
choose?

1 —

2 —

3 —

4 —

5 —

Do you have these shoes already? If not, where
are you going to buy them?

You can buy less expensive shoes, but, apart
from those lucky few whose feet will accommodate any covering, inferior shoes may cause
problems later.

When you get your new shoes home, spray
them with a shoe-protection agent and leave to
dry for a few hours. Then 'break them in',
wearing them around the house, first for a short
time and then for longer. The more comfortably
you and the shoes work together, the better you
will feel.

Keep two pairs of ordinary everyday shoes to
wear on alternate days, thus allowing the resting
shoes to 'breathe'. Always put shoe trees in shoes
whenever you take them off. Some people think
you should then leave the shoe trees in. Others
say trees need only be used for half an hour.
Covered-foam toes-only trees absorb perspiration, but they do not hold the shape of the heels
as well as the rigid-ended long-tailed trees. If you
have problems with smelly feet, use deodorizing
insoles. Clean the shoes regularly – don't wait for
them to become dirty. Damp leather is sensitive
to heat, so if the shoes are wet avoid harsh
drying. Stuff the toes with rolled orange-sized
balls of newspaper and allow to dry at normal
room temperature in a well-ventilated room.
Shoes made with materials other than leather
may also suffer from heat; crêpe soles can soften
and liquefy, and synthetic soling may 'balloon'.

Be prepared, too, for mending. Anticipate
when the heels are wearing down and go to a
reliable shoe repairer. Very thin or holed soles
allow footwear to flex excessively, throwing
increased stress on other components. Wetting
through thin or holed soles can ruin uppers, not
to mention being extremely uncomfortable.

(Good information on shoe care is available
from the Shoe & Allied Trades Research Association.)

Sweaters

This category includes jumpers, pullovers, gilets
and waistcoats (vests) – anything, in fact, which
is knitted, be it wool or not.

Fashion knitwear is one of the most exciting
developments in the last decade. Aside from the
wide range of patterns available to the home
knitter, there are shops which sell the work of
many small knitwear-designers. If you want to
save money on the less complicated styles, however, the universal advice is 'knit your own'.
Marjorie Littlejohn runs a highly successful
needlework store in Houston, Texas, and in
response to pressure from customers, allied with
her own acute fashion sense, she started to stock
knitting yarns a short time ago. She can barely
keep her polyester and silk ribbon yarns on the
shelves, they disappear so fast. She runs knitting
classes and says that her customers can make a
designer sweater for under half of what a ready-
made item would cost (see 'Make your own',
chapter 15).

Do not hang light-weight sweaters on clothes

hangers, as they might lose their shape. When you take a sweater off, lay it flat on your bed, fold it lengthwise into three, arms tucked in, and then fold it in half across its length.

The best method of storing such folded sweaters is on a shelf with the last fold facing you. Your sweaters will then be displayed as they are in shops. Do not pack them too closely, and do not put them in closed drawers, as your garments need some ventilation.

Larger and heavier-weight jackets can be hung from clothes hangers. To prevent them slipping off the hangers or mis-shaping, attach long tape loops to the shoulder/sleeve seams of the inside of each garment. The tapes will then go over the hanger's hook.

Woolite recommend a cold water wash. When handwashing, use the suggested amount of liquid or powder and soak garments for three minutes without rubbing. Rinse in cold water, roll in a towel to remove excess water. Do not wring or twist. Shape gently and dry flat, away from sun or heat. Similarly, follow their instructions for washing in a top-loading machine.

Tights and stockings

I do not think any man realizes how much money goes into a woman's leg covering. As soon as you put high-heeled shoes on – especially high-heeled sandals – your tights (pantihose) seem to snag, particularly at the big toe nail. One advantage of flesh-coloured tights, of course, is that at least the snag does not show so much!

As with lingerie, it really is worthwhile buying more expensive items. They generally last longer, as they are plain knit, as opposed to mesh, and are less susceptible to snagging due to their smoother texture. Your legs certainly look more elegant, too, so you feel better.

If you are wearing sandals – or slingback or toeless shoes – you need hose with sheer heels and toes. I find, alas, that these snag or ladder amazingly quickly: a little run seems to start just above my big toe nail ends, particularly if I am wearing high heels (the most durable seem to be 'L'eggs', if you can get them).

'One-size' tights can generally be worn by people of average size – although the definition of 'average' varies between different manufac-turers. Some tights do, however, have sizes printed on the packaging.

If you are tall and you find that the crotch of some tights tends to gravitate downwards during a busy day, simply wear a pair of underpants or light-control pants over your tights.

Wearing tights with panties attached elimi-nates the nasty seam-showing that otherwise happens if you are wearing a too-tight skirt or long trousers.

Whether you wear tights or stockings – which men find sexier and which many women prefer anyway – do wash your hose every day. Follow washing instructions on the packaging or use a soft solution like dishwashing liquid. Rinse thor-oughly and hang up to dry. Do not put hose in a washing machine, unless you want to run the risk of dyeing everything else in the load, and do not dry in a machine unless the hose is secured in a nylon laundry bag (see page 50).

Umbrellas

There are those who feel it is worth investing in a couture Burberry umbrella, who subsequently spend a lot of time worrying lest their treasure is stolen, lost, or turned inside out. A few years ago fashion expert Lee Rosati was in Harrods' trying to buy an umbrella that turned inside out and back again. She was told that no Harrods' um-brella ever turned inside out – but Lee lives in Buffalo NY where *all* umbrellas are often turned wrong way out by strong winds, so they must be able to be righted. She purchased a door mat instead (no, not to use in the rain – merely as a present).

The best value in umbrellas, in my view, is an unglamorous item with a loop attached to the handle. The latter is so that you can hang it up, and therefore see it more easily. The fact that it is unattractive will make it far less likely to be stolen.

(My favourite hotels, incidentally, are those that provide courtesy umbrellas in the rooms – like the Remington Hotel, in Houston.)

If you are interested in keeping up to date with trends in accessories, see the monthly magazine *Fashion Extras*.

CHAPTER 7

Special people's clothes

A few years ago people with unusual sizes had problems when it came to clothes. Today, if you have, say, a large bust or small buttocks, you still have to fend for yourself when it comes to shopping – or, if you are lucky, you can rely on a good salesperson or your fashion consultant. (Some pointers to help you are given in How *you can do it*, chapter 9.)

Fortunately for some, however, today many designers produce marvellous 'one size's that fit almost everyone. I find, for instance, that I can put on many Norma Kamali, Nicole Miller or Diane Freis designs without even having to look at the size first.

Regardless of whether you are tall or busty, big-shouldered or round-shouldered, if you feel you have an 'unusual' figure, look for loose-fitting garments which rely on emphasis on colour rather than cut or fit. Sometimes something in several different plain colours looks particularly striking.

Even short people can follow the above maxim – though they may have to shorten some of the garments!

For those with particular sizing and other clothes problems, here are some ideas and tips, in most cases from those who understand your predicament!

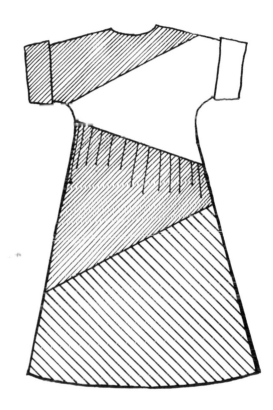

57 *A one-size three-colour dress bought in Manila from designer Backie Celdran.*

Bigger dressing

Chris Gillette is a former fashion model married to an American businessman. She enjoys good food and wine – and because she is a size 14 she started the Chrissy G range, which has sizes 14 to 20.

'The larger woman's first instinct,' she says, 'is to hide under camouflaging, tenty clothes. Very important, however, is the illusion of good proportion. This should include balancing the silhouette with the correct hairstyle and paying attention to your shoes.'

Christine Westwood owns SASSA (Sixteen And Several Sizes Above). She says: 'Once you know you can look glamorous and beautiful in good colours and shapes, it's much easier to make the decision and choose to be slimmer.'

She encourages the wearing of bold interesting colours and suggests that you forget about size labels and wear clothes which allow you to change size with them.

Another specialist in dress sense for larger ladies, Monica Flynn, says that grooming is particularly important. A tip she shares is that it is important 'never to squeeze into anything too small – nothing is more fattening'.

A few other pointers for larger ladies include:

1 If you have a large bust, never wear a plain back-fastening bodice: try to wear shirt-style dresses, diagonal stripes, vertical frills, long scarves, long beads, edge-to-edge jackets.

2 Balance big hips with plenty of interest at neck and shoulders and wear classic dresses that skim past waist and hips, or suits with long, loose jackets.

3 Tall, large, but well-proportioned women are fortunate: go for drama with large prints, swirling skirts, bat-wing sleeves and shawls (never try to fade away and minimize your size with tiny prints and apologetic colours).

4 If you are petite but, frankly, plump, you should try to look neat: choose the narrowest dresses you can find (if you have a relatively small waist, try princess line), plain if possible, or with small, smudgy prints, and avoid separates.

Sometimes those with big figures are embarrassed about going into shops; fortunately there are many good mail-order catalogues especially for them. Fashion Extra, for instance, is part of Marshall Ward (itself part of Great Universal Stores). Their catalogue, much recommended by Judith Chalmers, has a full range of clothes from Berkertex, Claudette, and other designers. It includes everything from evening gowns to track suits, with a full range of underwear and accessories. Many of their clothes, very reasonably priced, are attractive to any size – not only the 16+ for whom they are intended!

Dressing for the disabled

If you are in a wheel-chair you will find that jackets ride up so that the collar rises up your neck. Trousers seem to be similarly affected. Perhaps, alternatively, you have trouble getting

58 *Bigger women are often flattered by vertical stripes. This dress is available in sizes 16 to 26 from the Fashion Extra mail order catalogue.*

in and out of clothes. There is good help available for your particular dressing need: some addresses are given at the back of the book.

Gaining dressing

If you are putting on weight – and you are not pregnant (in which case see Pregnant, p. 72) – *stop immediately*. Why, in all honesty, let yourself be taken over by an expensive and miserable cycle of not being able to get into your clothes?

Loving dressing

All right, lovers, you wonder why you are sandwiched in between people who are putting on weight and those who are over a certain age? (You may, of course, fit into one or both of those other categories, but that is purely coincidental . . .)

All the points brought out elsewhere in the book apply to you, only in exaggerated form. You not only want to look your best – you want to look your *very* best. You need to feel so good that you forget completely about what you are wearing.

This is the time when you start looking at black suspender belts with red bows and, though you have not worn stockings since high school days, you will wear them now. He may buy you particularly sexy things or you may buy them for yourself. If things are bought for you, pretend they are just what you always wanted, even though you cannot believe he ever associated that particular design or cut with you.

This is also the time when you want clothes that take off quickly.

The Janin shirt and jacket are specially designed to suit your needs. The cut is front-opening without any cumbersome buttons or zips – it comes in various styles, but the distinguishing feature is that all are done up with real silk ties or with toggles.

Clothes at this time should make you feel ageless and sizeless – two important criteria behind the Janin shirt (address at back of book).

Middle-aged dressing

As fashion writer Natalie Allen says, 'If you can afford to buy quality clothes all the time, then I would be foolish not to advise you to do so; for as one matures, fewer, better clothes should be your rule.'

59, 60 *Versions of the versatile 'Janin jacket', with easy-to-undo toggle fastening (drawings by Su Quek).*

She suggests (for the over 40s):

(**a**) A sporty trouser suit is the natural replacement for too-tight jeans and carelessly co-ordinated tops, especially if you have any over-abundant curves to hide!

(**b**) No other combination has quite such a successful age-retarding effect as a well-cut blouson jacket worn with matching trousers and a snappy T-shirt.

(**c**) Remember that no matter how stylish the clothes, they will not work for you if your hair is badly groomed, your make-up out of date and your figure slack and/or overweight.

Other ideas to make you look younger include, from top to toe:

(**a**) A more natural hair-style with less spray.

(**b**) natural make-up

(**c**) clothes in pretty colours (not dull or mousey), soft feminine fabrics and a variety of textures

(**d**) Complementary co-ordinates rather than standard one-fabric suits

(**e**) Soft-falling jackets and dresses

(**f**) Carefully chosen accessories

(**g**) Slingback shoes.

Older dressing

Your figure may irretrievably alter as you get older. Some of my friends tell me that their waists have 'gone' and they have prominent 'saddlebags' around their upper hips. Whereas they used to be able to buy a standard size 12, now they need at least a size 14 dress, but it is going to be too large 'up top'.

The answer to this is either to buy that size 14 and put vertical pleats in from the shoulders down to the bust to make the garment fit properly – or to avoid one-piece items and go, instead, for separates. If you are worried about your changed figure, buy matching separates so that the eye of the beholder is not brought to the colour change around the waist.

You may find that front-opening garments are most comfortable – back zips and buttons can be particularly difficult to manage.

Try to keep as warm as possible. Wear scarves, gloves – and thermal underwear. If you have always worn stockings and never switched to tights (pantihose) you will find many chain stores now sell attractive suspender belts, although if you cannot wear anything constricting around your waist you may have to buy a liberty bodice and attach suspenders to it.

You can buy main garments from chain stores, who now appreciate the need for 'longer length' garments, but you will certainly be able to identify which of your friends have bought expensive items. The latest range of sheepskin coats, padded jackets and attractive daywear has the same snob-identification as designer garments to your younger relations.

In some ways your fashion sense adapts and you may no longer have 'every day' and 'Sunday best' clothes as you did in years past. It may be, however, that you will never adapt to trousers – although you may admit that, for practicality, they are sensible for gardening and general warmth!

Those who are really old have special problems – and I went to talk to Hilary Wharton, owner and director of Tyndale Residential Home in Yeovil. She suggests:

> Encourage older people to look well groomed and try to dissuade them from slopping around in slippers all day long. Boost their morale. Try to avoid a demeaning bib – a coloured apron is far less humiliating. If they sit a lot, think about woolly foot muffs in winter. Older people often love jewellery – and it does not have to be expensive.
>
> Wrap-around skirts are useful, as are Velcro (touch-and-close) fastenings, but if there are any buttons, sew them on a long shank or use two buttons sewn together with elastic to form a 'cuff-link'.
>
> You can buy split knickers/incontinence underpants. Hold up stockings with elastic tops, or suspenders linked together on a large buttonhole attached to the stocking before being pulled up and then fastened with one hand on to a button on the corset. Elastic shoe laces are a good idea.
>
> Among the many dressing aids available are long plastic sticks like coathangers with a curve at the end, and 'helping hand reachers' (like long claws), button hooks, dressing rails and plastic stocking 'gutters' (thin sheets of plastic attached to strings which open up stockings).

Party dressing
by Diana May

Party time should be fun time, not an ordeal to be endured now so that retrospectively you may consider it 'just about worth it'.

You need to attend the party in a truly positive

frame of mind, quietly confident that you look as nice as you can possibly manage and probably as pretty and elegant as anyone present. This will follow from careful clothes selection beforehand. It was Katherine Whitehorn who noted that there are three kinds of women – those who look effortlessly good no matter what, those who do not fuss about fashion and are superbly unbothered by it, and the vast majority of us, who *do* try but often limp through life uneasily aware that we have not quite succeeded at dressing well.

The trend in past years has been, when in doubt as to what to wear to a party, to under-dress rather than over-dress, but perhaps the pendulum is swinging back now, with the Princess of Wales' lead in daytime hats and evening gowns. It is crucial to think about the nature of the event to which you are going, and to reach some sort of decision about your intended clothes. You must then retain confidence in them all the time you are wearing them. If what you are wearing is clearly wrong and you cannot do anything about it, brazen it out: people will remember your face long after your odd choice of costume is forgotten!

What you should consider is:

(**a**) What clothes other people will be wearing (study past form, and the current invitation, for help on this);

(**b**) Whether you wish to be a 'clone' of the other women, or to be a little or a lot different;

(**c**) What you have in your wardrobe that fits the bill.

Long dresses make a woman feel like Scarlett O'Hara in her prime, but nowadays they are not worn so much and you are probably only safe wearing one when the invitation specifically says 'black tie'. If you do not want to wear a long dress or you are undecided, elegant evening trousers and a stunning top are suitable when others are wearing long dresses or short.

Do not be too daring. Remember, for instance, to temper your décolleté at your husband's firm's (or your own firm's) annual dinner-dance. You want to be remembered as someone in her own right, and not as someone who flashes bodily assets at one and all. If in doubt, dress up in something very simple and classic – dare I say 'the little black dress'? Wear a lush scarf, shoes and handbag, that are perhaps, unusual in shape or colour. Wear superb jewellery, whether real or fake. It is better to 'dress up' on such an occasion than to 'dress down'.

If you have managed to work out what other people are likely to be wearing, decide whether you wish to be different, and if so, how much? If you wish to show your contempt of fashion, dare to do so, but be prepared for the fashionable to be contemptuous of you. Try, otherwise, for a median choice of clothes, but lift it with individual touches by way of colour (Schiaparelli pink, for instance), make-up, hairstyle, jewellery and accessories.

The last big problem is how to ensure that you actually possess the right clothes for any party. Most women would consider that a wardrobe to take care of most parties requires:

2 long dresses

long skirt

short skirt in a special material

evening trousers in crushed velvet or similar

several tops that will go with either skirt or trousers (including a long-sleeved one for chilly houses)

several short dresses, some of which will double for daytime wear

smart suit for weddings

kaftans, kangas, etc., for casual and poolside parties

lightweight sandals or evening shoes

shawls and/or a fur jacket

evening bag (a shoulder bag is a good idea as you can forget about it as you stand at cocktail parties holding drinks and little canapes!)

For some parties, say street parties or roasting an ox on the village green, you will just dig deep into your 'regular' wardrobe, remembering that in Britain you can never underestimate how cold and wet it might be, and that dressing in 'layers' covers all eventualities.

A completely different category of party is the fancy dress occasion, which your invitation should specify. If you are not sure whether or not everyone will be in fancy dress, telephone the hostess as you do not want to be the only red-and-yellow jester in a room full of 'straights'.

Ideas on fancy dress can be gleaned from Jane Asher's *Book of Fancy Dress* (Pelham Books) or from local theatrical or fancy dress suppliers.

61 *Romantic silk organza ballgown with tiered skirt and pink faille sash, designed by David and Elizabeth Emanuel (makeup Barbara Daly, hair by John Frieda, photograph by David Bache, courtesy Emanuel).*

62 *Fancy-dress party outfit: a hip-length cardigan jacket is worn over a petticoat-topped ankle-length gown with elasticated hip 'divider' (the dress can be shortened later for normal wear). The back (shown shaded) can be cut as low as required.*

63 *Evening blouses by Hong Kong designers; pendant choker by Kai-yin Lo (photograph by Kevin Orpin, courtesy the Hong Kong Trade Development Council).*

Post-operative dressing

If you need special clothing at this time, you might like to contact some of the 'disabled' addresses at the back of the book.

Post-mastectomy patients will receive particular help from mastectomy associations and also from others who have had a mastectomy. Gillian Mann told me how after her operation she soon realized that she could wear swimsuits and other normal clothing: fortunately her sense of humour carried her through the time, for instance, when the 'stuffing' she put in her swimsuit swam out, and away, when she was bathing with friends one day. You need a lot of courage after a mastectomy. But the moral support of others will be of great help, so seek this support.

Pregnant and nursing dressing

This is especially a time to look your best and make you feel good. You should also try to always wear something that is *comfortable*.

For the first few months you should be able to wear your ordinary clothes, if they are not fitted at the waist. Then you should turn to garments that have fullness (of body, bust, skirt) as well as adjustable or elasticated waists.

Even if you do not normally wear a bra, you

64, 65 *Gone are the days when pregnant women had to wear smock-tunics over tight skirts with cut-out tummy panels. Now some future mums emphasize their girth with attractive dungarees, while others wear comfortable free-flowing dresses (photographs courtesy Mothercare).*

1 Dress Sense *applies to any age …. (photograph courtesy Dylon International).*

2 *The simplicity of this all-purpose, one-size shift with batwing sleeves is what makes it an invaluable addition to any woman's wardrobe (photograph courtesy The Limited).*

3 Opposite *Ideal workout clothes, with a short-sleeved leotard with flattering diagonal pattern and waist belt over footless tights (photograph courtesy Danskin).*

4 & 5 *Flattering necklines, courtesy AnnaBelinda, (left) and Marc Young (above).*

6 Opposite *Business-like neckline worn by Carol Jackson, founder of Colour Me Beautiful, photographed in front of her company's seasonal colour chart.*

7 *Colour, colour, in an outfit created and made by Jarmilla Gibbon of Croydon College. Starting out as painted and dyed white cheesecloth, a flowing multi-coloured smock is worn over a plain overbodice. There are strategically placed holes in the billowing sleeves through which the sleeve is pulled further to develop a mediaeval theme (hair by Sally at Simon Rattan, photograph by Eamon J McCabe, courtesy Dylon International).*

8 *Few could wear this and get away with it but if you do have the figure, it is for you! (photograph courtesy Danskin).*

9 *Old techniques in a new look: broderie anglaise and other needlework embellishment set into a stunning nightdress (photograph courtesy Marc Young).*

10 Below left *Travelling businesswoman starts the day …. (gown by Nicola Logan, make-up by Lancome, photograph courtesy the Inter-Continental Hotel, London).*

11 Below *Anyone could wear this cotton sweater designed and made by Alison Hill of Ravensbourne College of Art (hair and make-up by Rebecca at Pierre Alexander, photograph by Eamon J McCabe, courtesy Dylon International).*

12 Opposite *Plain colours have impact, as illustrated by these silk shirts from Yaufat in Hong Kong (photograph Harrison Tan, courtesy the Hong Kong Trade Development Council).*

13 *Clothes chosen for travel should always be comfortable, loose-fitting and simple as in this bell-sleeved top and co-ordinating trousers with unpressed pleats (photograph courtesy The Limited).*

14 *Clothes do not need to be expensive and formal to look chic. This casual T-shirt, unlined blazer and simple trousers combine perfectly to give an appearance of uncluttered elegance (photograph courtesy The Limited).*

will need good support at this time. Front-opening bras are useful as they can be worn later, when breastfeeding the baby. If it is your first baby, you should not need a maternity belt or corset as your abdominal muscles should be strong enough, but if you want support look out for pantie girdles with adjustable extra back support.

As your pregnancy progresses, you may need special swimwear: look out for garments with gathered tunic-type tops.

Wear shoes that feel comfortable. There is no reason why you should not continue to wear high heels until the last few weeks, by which time they may feel uncomfortable.

Packing to go into hospital to have your baby

What you need to have ready to take into hospital:

Mother:

3 bras
3 nightdresses
5 pairs of underpants

66 *Maternity swimwear by Playtex (photograph courtesy Playtex).*

1 bed jacket
1 tablet of soap
1 sanitary belt
2 face flannels
toothbrush and toothpaste
dressing gown and slippers
going-home clothes
telephone change

Baby

Large safety pins
1 box large-sized tissues
Going-home clothes

Later, when you are breastfeeding your baby, you will need clothes that disguise the extra weight you are still carrying, as well as ones cut to make feeding easy. Wash-and-wear clothes will make your laundry easier. Look for front-opening and nursing bras as well as front-opening nightdresses and blouses.

73

Short dressing

Freda Williams is just over five feet tall and has to cut several inches off all new coats and dresses. Similarly, all her petticoats need shortening (it is a good thing she can sew!).

'Unfortunately as I get older,' she says, 'my hips are broadening, and this causes even more problems as I have to buy larger sizes, and then there is even more shortening to do. The bust is often too large, too, so on dresses I have to put inverted pleats at shoulders.'

Shorter people who wear stockings can simply roll the excess over at the top. Those who prefer tights have more of a problem.

Sick dressing

Diana Hastings, author of *Home Nursing*, says that someone who is bedridden should try to look as pretty as possible in the circumstances.

> A nightdress is easier to manage than pyjamas, and since clothes tend to ride up when in bed the shorter the garment the better. Try to avoid man-made fibres. An attractive bedjacket makes the patient feel and look good, and it might provide some necessary warmth.
>
> If you are looking after someone who has been ill, get your patient out of bed as soon as you can and try to dress her in her usual clothes. This will certainly boost her morale.

Slimming dressing

When I first knew Carole Wesley she was – to put not too fine a point on it – a marvellous warm tank. She has now lost 170lbs. I asked her how she managed a 'changing wardrobe' as she slimmed.

> Most of the time I wore interchangeable separates and every three months, regularly, my dressmaker and I went through my wardrobe. If you really are on a 'long' slim, do not adjust your clothes too often. Try to do it on a regular basis.
>
> When I had lost 100lbs I actually bought my first new 'usual size' dress. What a thrill that was! For evenings, I had a long velvet dress with plain neck and long sleeves and it did not matter that it became looser every week.
>
> I bought new (and smaller) underclothes about every three months and simply did the fastening up on a tighter notch, or tied a knot in the elastic, in between.

67 *Practical student wear includes versatile separates – and lots of pockets! (courtesy British Home Stores).*

Student dressing

Kathryn Jarvis is reading geography at Sheffield University. She was wearing a mid-calf black 'tent dress' with turquoise neck scarf and black gladiator sandals when we met for a vegetarian lunch to talk about students and their clothes.

> The main thing [she said] is that students do not have a lot of money. Clothes therefore have to be as versatile as possible. You need things that you can wear every day, from morning through to night.
>
> It is a good idea to have clothes with pockets, for holding pens and keys and other things. Skirts are much more practical than trousers.
>
> People fortunately do not expect students to be smartly dressed. You do need at least a couple of semi-formal dresses, however – for a Hall ball or for going out for a meal.
>
> We tend to borrow each others' sweaters and a few other things. Laundry facilities in most Halls and college blocks are generally good, but it's best to avoid having any clothes that need dry-cleaning.
>
> Of course there are some students who are extremely well dressed and trendy. But no-one expects us all to look as if we have come out of a fashion magazine.

Tall dressing

Judy Rich is a six-foot-tall American who came to England in 1975 and could not find a thing – other than outsize – garments to wear. She therefore opened the first of her Long Tall Sally shops.

Judy feels tall women can wear more or less anything, and because they are tall they are *noticed*. They can go for dramatic effects and do full justice to brilliant colours. They are the ones who look best in trousers. But they should avoid schoolgirl collars, puff sleeves and anything that aims at a 'little girl' look.

Long Tall Sally sells clothes sizes 12 to 18 (sometimes 20). All are cut on longer than average lines, with measurements proportioned to fit comfortably: dress length 50in from nape of neck; skirt length minimum 30in; sleeves 26in long from shoulder seam; and trousers minimum 38in inside leg (left unhemmed).

Traditional dressing

James Ferreira, who has designed the 'travelling woman's wardrobe, in Around the world, chapter 12, says that there is definitely a trend among women from the Indian sub-continent towards traditional dress. And the sari, indeed, is often seen in Britain and elsewhere.

The sari is one length of fabric about $5\frac{1}{2}$ to 6 metres in length. Cotton and nylon are most commonly used, with silk reserved for more formal functions (very expensive gold embroidered saris are seen at weddings and important festivals). Most daily saris can be hand-washed.

The sari is worn with a short tight-fitting blouse (the choli) and an ankle-length underskirt. One end of the length of fabric is tucked into the underskirt and then wound around the body once. The middle is pleated into five or six vertical pleats and then the surplus fabric is taken round the back and over one shoulder.

An Indian resident in London tells me that, although beautifully elegant, the sari is not so useful in the humdrum city life around her now.

(It should also be mentioned that an executive secretary in Delhi told me that wearing the sari at work is difficult when you have to use a secretary's swivel chair: if you swivel in the wrong direction your clothing is likely to twist undone!)

Young dressing

Melissa Tuffley is 16 and has three younger sisters. She understands, therefore, how to dress older than young children and, at the same time, how not to look like mother.

Melissa told me that she and her friends definitely do not like to see older people wearing 'their' clothes:

We think it makes them look tarty and too young. It shows them off too much.

Girls of my age who are slightly overweight (like me!) prefer to wear middle-length skirts down to the calf with a petticoat underneath with the frills showing and either a shirt and a V-neck sweater or a T-shirt with a sweater or something over the shoulders. The people with better figures tend to wear more tight-fitting clothes.

Girls who are fashionable and do like to dress up usually feel more feminine in skirts. People who do not always like to wear skirts look and feel good in tight jeans (any colour!) and a very baggy jumper in a co-ordinating colour or a large plain shirt with the collar up.

By far the most important things in fashion to my friends and me are *accessories* – e.g. leg-warmers, fingerless gloves, scarves, bangles, hats, rings etc. Most people wear colours according to what suits them best but there are always definitely 'in' colours and it is important to be really up to date.

Those who have grown up out of children's clothes should have fun when dressing. They should *not*:

1 try to look like their mothers;

3 wear clothes too like their school uniforms;

3 buy clothes that are so expensive they have to be worn for ages to get good 'return'.

This is the one time in your life when you can mix inexpensive bought clothes with experimental 'do-it-yourself' ideas – and get away with them!

Some ideas for jazzing up an outfit include:

press-stud decoration

knitting sweaters and scarves out of leftover balls of wool (try mixing in some string, too) painting (uncooked!) macaroni and other pasta and threading them as jewellery

wear shirts as jackets

wear 2 shirts, one above the other

wear 2 scarves, 2 hats . . .

Don't worry what older people think. Sometimes they might even be envious that *they* cannot get away with it. Don't allow too many people to take photographs of you, though, as you will not be pleased, many years later, to see what a fright you looked when young!)

68 *Colourful options in 100% cotton calico: perfect for younger dress sense (courtesy British Home Stores).*

CHAPTER 8

Rites of passage

Something old, something new, something borrowed, something blue...

This is the one occasion in your life when all eyes will be on you. Some brides have their own dream dress imagined since childhood... but few seriously bother to think about the dress until the time comes near.

In traditional style, most brides still prefer a white dress – but there are so many *shades* of white. Diana May asked The Colour Company about 'what colour dress to wear'.

'If the bride chooses the right tone of white for her wedding dress,' said Kay Cornelius, 'It will complement her personal colouring to perfection.' Basing her selection on colour principles associated with various seasons, she suggests that 'winter' people should wear a brilliant white; 'spring' people might prefer an ivory white; 'summer' people should wear a soft white; 'autumn' people look good in oyster white.

The dress can be bought, hired, borrowed or made. Because the wedding dress is so important, it is advisable to look at as many dresses as possible.

Belinda O'Hanlon of AnnaBelinda is the designer whose marvellously romantic gowns have been worn at weddings all over the world. I asked Belinda for some tips. She said:

When choosing her wedding dress, all the bride should have to think about is what she will feel *happiest* wearing when everyone is staring at her.
It is *her* day. She should not necessarily think about what is fashionable. She should wear something that makes her feel her best.
Here are a few details to consider:

1 Does the design and shape suit height, figure and personality? Is it a dress in which she can relax and be comfortable (frills, bows and lace, for instance, or quiet simplicity)?

2 Is the colour right?

3 When choosing a fabric that suits the design and the bride, do not forget the time of year. Quilted bodices look silly in July, for instance, and chiffon is similarly out of place in December.

4 Choose the shape and general design first and then you will find it easy to concentrate on the details. Do you like the buttons, neckline and so on?

5 Do not forget the back!

6 Only when the bride has chosen what she wants to wear should she start thinking about head-dresses, veils, bridesmaids' dresses and flowers. After the main dress has been chosen everything else will simply fall into place.

My dress
by Sasha Wegrzyn

I decided to design my own wedding dress because I knew the style I wanted and what particular design suited me. I knew several designs and from them compiled the final concept. I found some fabulous material and although a dressmaker myself I decided to ask a friend to make it up for me.

We had several fittings in the early stages to check on size and length, with a final fitting to iron out any minor alterations required.

I was delighted with the finished result – it was rather nice knowing it was unique!

Accessories

Veils are popular with many brides – and here are some of the types available:

1 Antique lace veils are probably most expens-

69 *The back of a wedding dress is especially important, as this is what is seen as you pass down the aisle. Belinda O'Hanlon of AnnaBelinda pays special attention in many of her designs to tiny buttons, quilted panels and silk piping (courtesy AnnaBelinda).*

ive, and they may be rather heavy to wear. If you have fine hair the veil will have to be securely fastened with hairgrips (bobby pins) or a band or tiara.

2 Silk and tulle veils are light and easy to arrange and keep in place.

3 Nylon veils are least expensive, but they are rather slippery.

When you go to buy your veil do take along at least a sample of your dress fabric to make sure you get a complementary shade.

As far as *shoes* are concerned, you do not want to tower over either your father or your groom. You also may have to stand for quite a long time at the reception. Many brides opt for a low-heeled white shoe and, sensibly, 'break the shoes in' by wearing them around the house for some time beforehand.

If you do decide to wear spiky high heels, remember to check that there are no potentially dangerous open grills on the floor of the church as you proceed up and down the aisle. Check also that you will not be standing on grass at the reception – you do not want to sink in!

You are well advised to try on your *underwear* before 'the day'. Check that your bra's shoulder straps will not show (if they do, sew little tape retainers inside the dress's shoulder seams). Check that no 'lines' (e.g. top of tights) show through the white fabric.

If there is no place on your dress to hold a handkerchief, ask both your father and your groom to have a clean handkerchief in their pockets, in case you need one.

Remember hair and make-up must be perfectly complementary to your entire outfit. The Colour Company's Angel Nichol advises a 'winter' person to wear a dramatic make up using pinks and a 'summer' person to use English rose type colours, while 'autumn' and 'spring' people should perhaps go for rusts and coral colours.

(Many colour advisors, incidentally, offer pre-wedding consultations. Such advice makes a much-appreciated gift.)

Civil weddings

It is generally accepted that for a Register Office ceremony the bride wears something 'chic', maybe in white, with or without a hat. She certainly does not usually wear a long gown with train and veil.

Second marriages

If you are marrying in a church, the custom is to wear something simpler than the usual style, perhaps with a hat or headdress of flowers.

Going away

Traditionally, brides change into a special outfit before they leave their reception.

At Helena Cobban's wedding the guests were having such a good time that some did not even realize she and her husband were leaving for their honeymoon, and few saw Helena's 'going-away' dress until the photographs were developed.

The moral of this is that although you do want to 'look special' going away, your guests will probably not remember it too well, and you should definitely buy something that you will be able to use later. Unlike the wedding dress, which should be spectacular and will probably never be worn again, regardless of how many good intentions you have beforehand, the going-away outfit should have a practical future.

You might even choose to go away in something you already have. Jenny Myers of Farmington, Ohio, for instance, simply put her old green raincoat over her new going away dress – and it was written up in her local paper as a very special outfit!

In the past brides 'went away' complete with hat and gloves but, today, such accessories would be generally considered rather over-dressed.

Bridesmaids

No bride wants to be overshadowed on the greatest day in her life, but she may well wish to surround herself with good friends or relatives to complement her image. The line-up may consist of two or three older bridesmaids – married ones will be called 'matrons of honour' – and/or child bridesmaids or pages. Although these little ones may look angelic, it is good to remember the old actors' advice to be wary of working with children or animals as they can steal the show!

The adult bridesmaids will certainly wish to wear their dresses again for dances and other special events, so do co-operate with them on choice of design and material. Try to choose a style that will suit their differing figures and colouring: try possibly to choose something that can be scaled down to suit child attendants.

Many today buy dresses in varying sizes from a chain store, rather than going to the expense of having dresses made.

The bridesmaids will probably offer to pay for some of the cost: some brides compromise and give the dresses and flowers if the attendants will pay for similar shoes. The groom traditionally gives all the attendants a gift, say a necklace or bracelet that can be worn with the outfit.

Mother of the bride or groom

This is a long day for the mothers. Do not exacerbate the situation with a sneaking feeling of dissatisfaction with your outfit...

Choose something in which you will feel comfortably right. You want more than anything on this day to be able to 'forget' what you are wearing so that you can give all your attention to the wedding party. At the same time, you want to be confident that you are one of the best-dressed women of your generation at the festivities.

Do check colours with the bridesmaids' outfits and, also, with what the other mother is going to wear. You will both appear in the photographs.

It seems customary in some areas to wear a dress and jacket, a dress and coat, or a suit. A dress by itself, however, may well be younger-looking. If you choose a hat with a big picture brim, make sure that you can still comfortably greet guests with a kiss without knocking the hat askew.

Wear comfortable shoes and carry an unobtrusive bag (for handkerchief, just in case, and change to put in the church funds).

Wedding guests

You should not upstage the principal figures at the wedding but this is, nonetheless, a time when you too can luxuriate in an occasion for elegant dresses and, perhaps, fantastic hats.

You do not necessarily have to wear gloves. You should avoid any outfit that is mainly black – considered by some to be bad luck – and, because you may not know whether the reception is being held on grass or in a hot or cold room, make sure you wear shoes that do not have spiky heels, and if you are likely to feel the cold have a wrap handy.

70 *Wedding guest outfit, designed and sketched by James Ferreira.*

Christenings

Apart from family and the godparents, you should simply dress as you would normally for church. Check beforehand whether other women will be wearing hats.

If you are mother or grandmother, you might at least like to wear a hat. Make sure it does not have such a large brim that your face is hidden in photographs. If you are likely to be holding the baby avoid dangly earrings (if he is a few months old) and, similarly, avoid wearing fabric that will show marks and later require professional cleaning.

Funerals

Do not overdress. This is a sad time for everyone concerned but try, if you can, to find out what the family are wearing.

71 *If you want to wear a veiled hat, check that you have one, like this, that allows you to push the veil up in order to kiss the bridal party and eat and drink with ease! (courtesy British Home Stores).*

If they are simply going to wear fairly sombre clothes and no hats, you would look out of place turning up in large black veiled hat, black suit and black stockings.

Remember to have money handy as there is often a collection for the church or chapel. And remember, too, to have a clean handkerchief. If you are going on to a wake or other occasion afterwards, have make-up handy so that you can 'repair your face' after the funeral.

CHAPTER 9

Work clothes

Working women need to look chic, business-like and thoroughly in charge of their particular situation.

You need to put on clothes – and then forget about them. You should dress suitably to your own work environment.

If you are a personal assistant in a film production company, for instance, a comfortable jersey 'jump suit' might be much more suitable than a sombre dress with court shoes (which *would* be more the mode of dress if you were an executive in a bank).

Martine Borgemeister, in her busy life as a sales and public relations executive in one of the world's leading champagne houses, says that she usually has one suit for summer and one for winter and a combination of jackets and skirts which can be combined with each other to form a number of outfits. 'I do tend to buy expensively,' she admits, 'mostly because the cheaper clothes do not usually appeal to me – they do not usually last as long or keep their shape. My clothes have to be hard-wearing because I buy few and wear them often.'

Gloria Higgins, Director of Fashion for Aparacor in the United States, feels strongly that working women must try even harder to dress correctly for their role: 'You cannot take for granted that you will be accepted on your talents alone: you must look the part as well.'

In a political world, for instance, many ambitious women follow the basic rules of the successful legislative look. As John T. Molloy, author of several books on 'dressing for success', says, 'the more power involved, the more conformity you are likely to have'.

So, women who want to succeed in Washington DC, for instance, are advised to keep away from flashy colours, greens and browns (perhaps too casual), red shoes and 'designer labels'. They are going to present a more effec-tive picture if they wear black, grey, navy blue and low-heeled closed-toe shoes.

Look professional

Think of Andora, wearing a cardigan over a tight, low-necked blouse, tight short skirt and high heels.

Now think of Pandora, wearing a well-cut jacket over a shirt with bow at the neck, an ample skirt that covers her knees and well-cleaned medium-height heels. Who looks the most professional, Andy or Pandy?

Rules that working women might find handy include:

1 If you are ambitious, always dress at least one step up the career ladder.

2 Avoid large-print fabrics and garish colours.

3 Always dress to a similarly high standard.

4 Invest in good accessories (shoes, belts, bag).

5 Do not overdo make-up or wear too much clanking jewellery.

Look yourself

There is no point in trying to dress like your male colleagues. Pin-striped trouser suits, flat shoes and no make-up do not impress. They *threaten*. Well-cut feminine, though not frilly, clothes are less aggressive to male colleagues. If you dislike skirts try a compromise – culottes.

Carol Wood, Public Relations Officer for Sheraton Management Corporation (Europe, Africa, Middle East and South Asia) told me:

'I never wear trousers for business. There is no point in throwing away the advantages of being a woman without gaining any of the advantages of being a man. With all the fun of being feminine, it seems ridiculous to imitate men.'

72 *Marvellously practical black jersey work suit from the Emanuel collection (photograph courtesy the Emanuels and Lynne Franks).*

73, 74 *Executive separates by Thomas Wee of Singapore (sketches by Su Quek).*

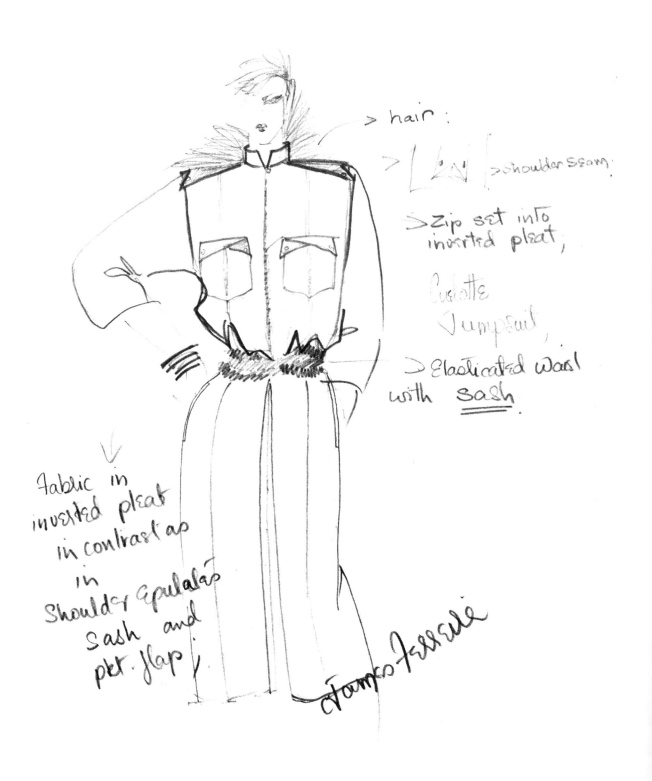

> hair :

> [L☐N] >shoulder seam.

> zip set into
inserted pleat,

Culotte
Jumpsuit,

> Elasticated wool
with sash.

Fabric in
inserted pleat
in contrast as
in
Shoulder epulates
sash and
pkt. flap.

Gianfranco Ferré

At work

Avoid anything too tight, revealing or overtly sexy when you are at work.

If you are likely to come into contact with foreign business associates it is particularly important to avoid too unfeminine a look. New York based banker Irene Woo, for instance, says that her international clients are completely taken aback by a blue-suit and bow-tie clone.

(Femininity, of course, is taken by people in different parts of the world to mean different things. Those working in Iranian-owned banks around the world are at the very least encouraged to cover their hair, if not even more.)

Once you have made your clothes selection for the day, try to forget what you are wearing. If your tights (pantihose) ladder, try not to be constantly looking down at them in the middle of your finance planning meeting. When you can discreetly go to the ladies' room, change into the fresh pair you should always have in your desk.

Never, never, do your make-up in public.

After work

Sometimes there is no clear distinction between daytime and after hours clothing. And it happens all too often, anyway, that it is impossible for you to change before 'going out'.(Occasionally you run into real problems. I delivered this book to the publishers – in Central London – on the way to Glyndebourne. A prize is offered to the most imaginative suggestion of how I coped with this problem!)

Generally it is possible simply to 'dress up' your daytime clothes. If not, you may be able to change in a ladies' room or in your car.

Here are a couple of tips for daytime to evening:

(a) Wear a black suit by day and simply remove the blouse or shirt for the evening.

(b) If you have been wearing a shirtwaist in the office, undo a few buttons and put on higher-heeled shoes to take you on to the evening engagement (if in doubt as to how many buttons to undo, play safe: it is always easier to undo a button in a restaurant than to do one up!).

In preparation for any evening event, always have emergency supplies in the office (see p. 88).

75 Practical business dress, with culotte skirt, specially designed and sketched by James Ferreira.

Be individual

Whatever happens, do not aim to dress exactly like all the others. I remember staying in a hotel a few years ago when a big business convention was going on and I seemed to be the only woman in sight not wearing a well-cut two-piece suit with burgundy high heels and the ubiquitous briefcase!

It is easier to express individuality as you gain confidence in your ambitious progress. Maryann Keller, for instance, who manages stock portfolios at Vilas-Fischer Associates in New York, says that the first thing she wanted when she started earning a decent income was a Missoni dress! If you cannot afford a Missoni, or it is not to your taste, nonetheless do try to personalize your business outfit, perhaps with a pretty scarf or an unusual colour combination.

Pregnant at work

All the same pointers that apply to other future mothers apply here (see chapter 7). Some regular maternity clothes may be suitable – or you can look in *Working Woman* to get names and addresses of suppliers of clothes specially with you in mind.

Other work styles

Most of the information above is aimed at 'executive dressers': those for whom the picture they present is directly associated with work ambitions.

Other working women have their clothing styles dictated for them (policewomen, nurses and the military, for instance). And some need work clothes that are primarily protective (engineers, agriculturalists and many factory employees).

It may be that if you cannot express your personality at work you compensate, in your leisure hours, with especially feminine or eye-catching clothes.

You should condition yourself not to hate your impersonal work clothes. Think positively. You save a lot of time – and money – by being spared the question facing 'executive dressers' who have to begin every working day with 'what shall I wear?'!

Supplies

Shopping can be a problem for executive women

who are short of time. Some mail-order companies like Royal Silk and Selective Marketplace specifically offer 'business' clothes. Alternatively, busy women may find it easiest to use shopping services (see chapter 14).

It is a good idea, incidentally, to keep some 'first aid' items in the office, e.g.:

raincoat
umbrella
cardigan
spare tights

76 *This black Gucci suit goes from working day to evening; in the office, it is worn with a blouse that is removed before the fun begins (make-up by Lancôme, photograph courtesy the Inter-Continental Hotel, London).*

make-up set
pair of high-heeled shoes
evening bag

Help for working women can be obtained from Career Guild, Emily Cho and Colour Me Beautiful (addresses at end of book).

CHAPTER 10

Exercise clothes

There is nothing better than having the right equipment – and that includes clothing.

One of the main complaints of those who run, jog, play tennis etc. today is that not all garments are easy-care. A London girl who runs regularly, for instance, says that by the end of the week she probably has seven different sets of garments ready to launder/clean and many of those require hand-washing or other special attention. This is time consuming, and expensive on her pocket. (The moral to this story is to read washing instructions on labels attached to the insides of all garments before you buy.)

Those in the United States are better off. Sports clothes are often much more attractive, cost less to buy and are certainly much easier to look after.

Fortunately, some garments are designed by those who wear them, and they understand the maintenance problems.

Lynn Tan, for instance, is a bubbly 27-year-old Singaporean who, when studying technical design, bumped into the figure-hugging 'leotard' business by accident. Her family boutique sold imported negligées and underwear, and on one of her own trips abroad she saw some exercise outfits which she thought were 'smashing'. Because of the problems of importing, high cost and stock surplus, she thought about producing locally. Today, with her four sisters, she is busily into production.

Those who produce good workout clothes understand the responsibility of encouraging people to exercise correctly. The international firm Danskin, for instance, have joined forces in Britain with the Imperial Society of Teachers of Dancing (ISTD) to co-produce a 'Body focus poster' which illustrates the ISTD's safe exercise/dance programme. With a grounding of dance movement and jazz techniques, Body Focus routines tone the body and enhance the capacity of heart and lungs. (If you want to know more about the Body Focus method, send a large stamped addressed envelope to the address at the back of the book.)

Danskin's own range of workout clothes is unendingly varied – in Houston's Galleria the other month I was impressed by the leotards with little puffed sleeves, the wrestler's 'pants with straps' and the shiny leather-look garments. A good leotard should stretch when you do and spring back to second-skin shape.

For the beginner, a good workout wardrobe could consist of:

plain black short-sleeved leotard

black tights (footless, but with under-arch/shrimp strap)

overdress for cooling down

headband

legwarmers

'aerobic' shoes.

'Aerobic' shoes – also used for jazz exercise and other high-movement exercising – should be lightweight and with flatter soles than, say, tennis shoes. They are made by many of the big sportswear companies.

As far as other sports are concerned, if you are a beginner you should *not* immediately invest in the 'entire works' that you may need if you continue seriously in that activity but which otherwise might be wasted ... memories of my own sortie into golf spring to mind: I bought a set of clubs, bag, umbrella and sun and rain clothing. My golfing lasted two months and all the specially purchased items but the umbrella had to be diverted to other purposes.

Some sports do, of course, require basic rudiments in order even to start. If you are riding, you need a hard hat and boots. If you are going

77 *Leotards by Lynn Tan, sketched by Su Quek.*   **78** *Fashion for fitness by Danskin.*

to play tennis or squash you need appropriate racket and shoes (and note that each sport has special shoes and you should not, for instance, wear trainers for badminton or tennis shoes when playing squash). Whatever your sport, you need warm-up clothes for pre-sport and after-sport wear (a track suit will double, also, as a jogging outfit). You also need the right type of support bra, and G-string underpants are ideal (see 'Underwear and accessories', chapter 6).

In the main, as with the exercise clothes mentioned at the beginning of this chapter, garments available in America are probably going to be more easily maintained than those purchased elsewhere. Some of the chain stores in Britain have good tennis and other sports clothes but only in the appropriate season. If you play all year round, or if you travel, you will probably have to pay more to buy required garments at a more pricey store.

79 *A diagonal seam gives a truly professional feel and fit to workout clothes: the high cut-away leg is flattering (photograph courtesy Danskin).*

80 *Sports clothes should be chosen for comfort: this tennis dress has an elasticated waist and it is worn with a fleecy lined gilet (photograph courtesy British Home Stores).*

81 *Practical cover-ups/jogging suits (photograph courtesy British Home Stores).*

82 *Special supportive and/or no-seam bras are available for sports enthusiasts (photograph courtesy Playtex).*

CHAPTER 11

Holiday clothes

Holidays constitute problems all of their own. Where are you going, and how and for how long? You will probably find that you need as much for a two-night stay at a friend's house as you would for two weeks in a foreign hotel.

Packing

There are, to my mind, four levels of packing:

1 Travelling by car, in which case you might be able to lay clothes, on hangers and in plastic bags, straight on to the back seat.

2 Plenty-of-room suitcase packing, with hanging clothes in plastic bags and using the traditional method of masses of tissue paper to protect everything. This method of packing takes up a lot of suitcase space.

3 If you do not have that amount of space, try making parcels or swiss rolls. Full length items I lay one at a time, full length out on a bed (or clean floor), folded from shoulder to hem so that the 'shape' is about 40cm wide. Another similarly folded garment is placed on top, and so on. When all the shapes are thus forming a multi-decker sandwich, I carefully roll, starting from the shoulders down to the hem. The resulting swiss roll shape can be put in a plastic bag – pierced to allow it to breathe – or placed directly in the suitcase.

Small items like blouses can be carefully folded into envelope-like packages and placed one above the other in your case. Shoes, belts and other unusually shaped items can be placed in plastic bags, again pierced.

4 If you are *really* short of suitcase space, eschew all plastic bags and pack items individually, even putting make-up into small plastic travelling pots. These can be slotted in, around shoe heels and so on, and you can get a lot more into the case using this method . . .

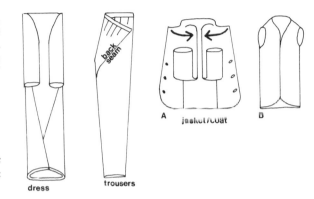

dress   trousers   A   jacket/coat   B

83 *Fold main garments so that they are about 40cm wide: jackets and coats are folded right sides together (A) so that the sleeves are inside the shape (B).*

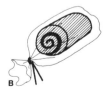

84 *Lay shapes one on top of the other, the longest at the bottom. Roll as a sausage (A) and place in a plastic bag (B).*

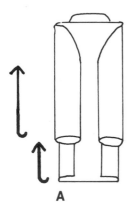 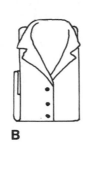

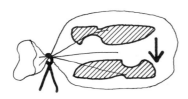

85 *Shirts can be folded upwards from the back (A) to look as they do when newly bought (B). Shoes can be put inside plastic bags.*

However you pack, the important thing to remember is to try and keep the level of packed goods as even as possible. This way, you will be able to get much more in your case.

What to take

Here are some checklists of what you might need to take with you, on work or holiday.

Long-distance packing

The basic overseas packing list below assumes you are flying. It will take you round the world and cope with most unforeseen occasions. (NB. You can write in your own extra requirements in the space provided.)

beige classic raincoat with removable lining

folding umbrella

black shawl

....
....

well-cut black lightweight wool suit (jacket can be worn separately)

black silk baggy trousers and long-sleeved long tunic top

white cotton trousers and matching long-sleeved white shirt

silk or thin polyester jersey dress

brightly coloured plain polyester shirtwaist to wear as dress or over trousers

densely patterned cotton dress

batik wrap skirt

black and white cotton jersey T-shirts

....
....
....
....

?tennis dress

?bikini

one-piece swimsuit with matching kanga(s)

lightweight kaftan (doubles as dressing gown/beach robe)

4 bras

4 pairs panties

full-length slip (doubles as nightgown)

selection of tights, out of packets and in plastic bag

....
....

black canvas day bag with shoulder strap

small black evening bag, clutch with optional shoulder strap

couple of plastic bags to hold shopping and wet swim clothes

standard black belt

silk scarf

long brightly coloured chiffon scarf

high black sandals, backless

low black peep-toe walking shoes

flat white sandals

gold slippers (double up as evening/night footwear)

white trainers/tennis shoes

....
....

86 *Kangas are really versatile:* one *can be knotted at shoulder and hip (left drawing):* two *can form a dress and shoulder bag (right drawing), and if you have* three *you can form skirt, bodice (folded diagonally, crossed in front and knotted at back) and turban (folded diagonally, twisted and tied).*

hairdryer
travel iron   dual voltage

enough make-up

enough pills to last the entire trip + 5 days

aspirin

scissors

small knife

length of string

small supply of elastic bands and paperclips

pens, pencils and paper

corkscrew

....
....

Remember always to take along a roll of plastic bags – and it is a good idea, too, to slip in at least one lightweight plastic hanger.

Do not forget to take some *holiday reading*. Barbara Hardwick of Weight Watchers says her favourite holiday reading would be:

1 Any Jeffrey Archer.
2 *War and Peace.*
3 Somerset Maugham short stories.

Weekend packing

This is a British two-night weekend packing list, assuming you are travelling by car:

beige raincoat

short padded jacket

....
....

selection of 2 of:
suit with skirt
suit with pants
long-sleeved dress
short-sleeved dress

long skirt/kaftan

blue jeans

skirt

co-ordinating shirt

co-ordinating sweater

....
....

?sports clothes

2 bras

2 pants

dressing gown

nightdress

3 prs tights/stockings

daytime bag

evening clutch

scarf

belt

evening/best shoes

daytime shoes

slippers

rubber boots

gloves

make-up

....
....

87 *Comfortable go-anywhere separates are good travellers'
aids (separates available sizes 16–26 from the Fashion
Extra mail order catalogue).*

One-night packing

For an overnight stay, carrying a small hand-tote:

clothes you have on (including coat/raincoat)

umbrella

change of main garments (say another easy-care dress)

thin shawl/wrap

nightgown

lightweight dressing gown

bra

panties

tights

bare essentials of make-up, with minute quantities of heavy items put into little plastic containers

....
....

When you arrive

When you arrive, do not worry if your clothes are horribly creased. Hang the garment you want to wear first on your plastic hanger. Put it

88 *Country weekend clothes by Aquascutum: a showerproof polyester/cotton jacket is lined with house check to match shirt, wool trousers and cap (courtesy Aquascutum).*

on the shower rail in the bathroom and turn the shower on, as hot as possible and full blast (make sure that the water does not reach the garment – and make sure the plug hole is unblocked!)

If you find you have forgotten something, try not to panic. If you are staying in another house for a weekend, it is quite likely that you can borrow what you need. If you are on holiday or business away from home, you should be able to buy what you want.

I arrived in Manila, Philippines, a short time ago and it was hot. My Norma Kamali cotton jumpsuit was black and it had long sleeves . . . I nearly boiled. Fortunately Manila has some tremendous new designers and I was taken round to the home office of a paediatrician's wife, Backie Celdran, and within literally five minutes I had bought a stunning and really versatile loose cotton smock.

Sometimes you pack not necessarily to go on holiday, for example packing to go into hospital to have a baby, see p. 73 in 'Special people', chapter (7).

CHAPTER 12

Around the world

Living overseas

Those who live overseas may have special problems. In Saudi Arabia and some other areas, for instance, you should always wear long sleeves and try generally to show as little of your body as possible. In Malaysia, avoid wearing yellow, the 'royal' colour. In Japan, in order to compete with 'the locals', you should have an extensive wardrobe (one survey maintains that the average Japanese woman has a wardrobe of at least 100 skirts, blouses and other outerwear). If you are posted to Houston, you will need as much jewellery as possible and you will have to give attention to couture and excellent grooming and make-up.

If you are going to live overseas, try to find out beforehand what clothes you will need and what you should avoid. If you are with a large international company, information will probably be readily available from your personnel officer. If you are going to such places as Hong Kong, there are good 'welcome' booklets published by the American Women's associations that tell you what you need to know.

Remember, incidentally, that sometimes clothes you have *made* overseas look all right in country of origin but may seem out of place when you get back home. (As long-term Canadian diplomat Janice Sutton says, 'You can always tell someone who lives overseas by her *real* jewellery and her *home-made looking* clothes!'

Travel overseas

Few people travel with hairdressers and maids. Some travel with hairdryers and a small iron. Others do not have space for either – or time to use them anyway.

Maryann Keller used to travel widely as an analyst for Paine Webber. In one year she went to Japan four times and within the space of nine weeks she made four return trips across the Atlantic. 'Silk dresses are very light,' she said, 'they hang out wrinkle-free if you pack them right and you can put a jacket over them to change the look.'

I agree with her. Increasingly I find one-piece clothes rather than separates better for business travelling, particularly if garments co-ordinate.

James Ferreira has designed a compact 'executive travel wardrobe' for *Dress Sense*. He is 27. Born into a family of professional sportsmen in Bombay, Jimmy (as he is always called) always knew that he wanted to be a fashion designer. 'When I was little, I always used to get myself invited to every wedding in town, just so that I could see what the bride wore!' After working with Zandra Rhodes in London, he returned to India. He designs for films, for film stars and, in particular, for women with style who want ageless, classic, go-anywhere garments.

He works exclusively in natural fabrics, mainly pure cotton but also some raw silk. His clothes all pack flat, folded as envelopes or parcels. Aware of the traveller's needs, he includes lots of pockets (for holding boarding cards, keys and other essentials). Waists are all elasticated to allow for girth expansion that often comes with air travel, and his skirt lengths are long enough to allow you to bend over to put things on your little luggage trolley without revealing your 'all'.

This special travel collection will take you anywhere. Most of the garments can be layered. I specially like the simple wrap-over dress that can be worn loose or, as illustrated, with a belt. By day, wear it with its own button-on front modesty 'bib', differently coloured each side so that it can blend with the dress or deliberately contrast. By night, remove the bib altogether. (Jimmy's address is at the end of the book.)

Poplin Dress
with
wrap over front
panel with
loose
button down
bib

Button down double
lined loose bib one
side contrast.

Straight wrap over
front panel dress
worn with suede
assimetric Belt.

Fully lined in Contrast
with hidden pads

Shirtlike Blouse

Forward forward
Jacket;

Poplin Dress
(Wrapover)

V
in seam
pockets;

Emb Voile
Blouse;

Cotton Satin
+
Voile Gadget (pleat)
skirt.

Emb Voile one side
wing collared blouse
worn with.

89, 90, 91 *Executive travel wardrobe specially designed by James Ferreira. A short jacket is worn above a wrap-over dress with button-on bib that can be removed for more formal evening wear. Also shown is another dress in embroidered voile. All the garments have handy in-seam pockets for carrying tickets, coins and so on, and all have elasticated waists.*

Personal notes

Here are a few ideas, from my own personal notebook, for overseas dressing and shopping in some countries other than Britain, Canada and the USA. (Further and more detailed information can be obtained from Mary Gostelow Enterprises.)

Australia – business girls often literally wear the trousers . . . and people of all sizes wear shorts. Many people need three different wardrobes (winter, summer, autumn), and with the increasing patriotic fervour for home products, many of the clothes are Australian. Popular shops include David Jones and Grace Brothers, and, for younger women, Sports Girl, Stock Jeans and Katies are popular.

Anyone travelling to Australia is advised, generally, that daytime wear is more informal than in Britain but evening wear is slightly more formal.

Austria – buy coats and suits and, also, fine work on white and other blouses.

Finland – two marvellous shops in Helsinki are Stockmann's (a giant department store which supplies goods to diplomats and others in hardship posts around the world) and Marimekko, good for fabrics and attractive wear-anywhere bright cotton clothes (expensive, however).

France – this is where you can buy that well-cut shirt, skirt, dress, or pair of trousers that will *always* look good quality. Martine Borgemeister has shopped extensively in Canada, Britain and in France:

> For the kind of clothes I buy I do not consider France to be more expensive than Britain. Evening wear, on the other hand, is especially hard to find and is expensive. For the woman who has to entertain at formal ceremonies, this can be very costly: the shops seem only to be aiming at the very rich.
>
> I find French women wear more make-up than the English, despite the fact that I do not think French men are any fonder of sticky lipstick than the Englishman is! Shoes are important: I usually

92 *From Hong Kong designer Patricia Chong, elegant silk jacquard dresses with elaborate appliqué shawl wraps (photograph Gerry Gokson, courtesy the Hong Kong Trade Development Council).*

buy a neutral colour that goes with everything but is good quality, and then if there is any money left over I might get something a little more fancy . . . the same with other accessories.

Germany – clothes are generally tremendously well made. Look out for good winter coats and suits – and anything in leather. Not good for sweaters or full-length slips. One of my favourite stores is KdV (car-de-vay) in Berlin.

Greece – excellent design on lots of cotton outfits (go for design-for-now rather than longevity of garment's existence).

Hong Kong – one of the world's greatest shopping areas. There are factory outlets, galore – places like Four Seasons and Maytag where you can buy 'international designer names' garments at a fraction of the usual cost. Look out, too, for some of the local designers' work – Patricia Chong, Eddie Lau and their colleagues. Everywhere, too, you can buy bags and belts (including spurious designer names). Warning: if you are of even average height do *not* expect to be able to get dresses long enough – or shoes big enough!

India – buy silks, shoes (in Bombay, go to the Oberoi Towers Hotel's shopping arcade or, if you can brave public streets, go to Metro, behind the Taj Mahal Hotel).

Italy – buy Italian designer clothes at much less than anywhere else. The area at the bottom of the Spanish Steps in Rome is an especially good shopping ground, but do not be waylaid by those selling spurious items on the Steps themselves.

Malaysia – best for shoes, which I always try to buy when there. (Look for Windy designs in the Metro store.)

New Zealand – unlike Australia business women here would not generally wear trousers, but well-cut skirts or suits. No coat required, but anyone travelling to New Zealand should bring a jacket and warm woollens for winter, and lots of light-weight clothes for summer; mix-and-match separates are always best. Formal evening wear is short, with nice jewellery. Many prefer never to wear tights or stockings. Younger people enjoy wearing very high-heeled shoes!

Philippines – buy brightly coloured straw designer handbags, especially those designed and made by Cora Jacobs for Yves St Laurent, Bloomingdales and so on. Also, my favourite ready-to-wear designers are Rusty Lopez and Backie Celdran.

Portugal – buy T-shirts and leisure wear.

Singapore – new designers are always springing up, it seems, in the many multi-storied shopping plazas along and off Orchard Road. One of the most talented I have come across for a long time is Thomas Wee, a self-trained designer in his late thirties, who sewed his first garment when he was 12. His clothes are versatile, yet simple and elegant, with great emphasis on details, balanced lines and excellent finish. His retail line is exclusive, but he also designs a mass market range which is sold in Germany, Australia and the Middle East.

Spain – good value in belts, bags and shoes, and also in fringed shawls. Shops to look out for include El Corte Ingles and Galerias Preciados.

Sri Lanka – Barbara Sansoni's ready-to-wear range is breathtaking. Barbara, whose 100% cotton furnishing fabrics come in mouthwatering colours, designs traditional classic garments. Her colleague Esmé designs such 'originals' as the Esmé coat, a voluminous hip-length jacket with its fullness caught into an edgeband – and into tiny wrist cuffs.

Thailand – those Bangkok stitchers can copy anything. For plausible copies of up-to-the-minute couture clothes at knock-down prices, go to boutiques in the Siam Center (Jaspal's, Space and so on). If you must stick traditionally to the Thai silk so popularized by Jim Thompson, look at the many silk boutiques which still 'make up in under 24 hours', in all the big hotels.

United Arab Emirates – super spangled evening sweaters and jackets and really versatile cotton 'dressy' separates from Helen Alexander's Amazing Grace showroom in Dubai.

USSR – if you have left anything behind when you get there on holiday, forget it, comrade – it's impossible to buy *anything* suitable (even deodorant), so before you leave home, double-check everything.

CHAPTER 13

Money and clothes

I have deliberately followed this chapter, on money, with one on shopping, for without careful management of the former, you cannot successfully embark on the latter. This chapter therefore discusses how much to spend on clothes – and what type of shopping is best for you.

Paying for clothes

You can pay with cash or by cheque, traveller's cheque, charge card (American Express or Diners Club), credit card (Access, Trustcard or Visa) or with a shop account card.

Shops sometimes offer different types of accounts:

(**a**) A *charge account* means that you are invoiced at the end of, say, every month for all items charged during that period, and you are expected to pay the whole amount promptly.

(**b**) A *budget account* means that you automatically pay a certain amount to the shop at regular intervals and you are allowed credit up to a stated level: sometimes you are behind, sometimes you are ahead.

(**c**) A *credit account* means that you are given credit up to a certain limit. You do not have to pay the whole amount owing each month, but you will be charged interest on the unpaid amount.

Do check and compare the interest rates charged by different shops and credit card companies.

You need help?

No-one can tell you how much you should spend. It is up to you to work out for yourself what is right for your budget. If you need help, talk to your bank manager – he or she is not nearly such an ogre as you might imagine.

If you need a loan to enable you to put together an entire wardrobe, say to start a new job, make an appointment to talk to your bank manager. See on what terms he could help you. Then study the terms of accounts at shops that you like. Work out what is going to be the least expensive method of borrowing money and go for that – though you should bear in mind that if you decide to 'borrow' with a shop account you are restricted to buying in that shop.

Your budget

Try keeping an annual record of everything you spend on clothes, including tights. Is the final figure a shock? Could you have done better?

Without working out a plan like the basic wardrobe in chapter 3, you will undoubtedly spend more money, and spend it on items that cannot take such an important role in your dressing schedule.

How much to spend overall is a personal and unique problem which takes into account your kind of life (business more expensive than home-based), age (generally, young adults spend more than their elders), location (south, north, city or country) and personal connections (entrées into discount shopping), as well as the ceiling imposed by available income.

The key to the whole concept is *value for money*. If you wear something enough times, its unit cost per wearing comes down and down. Burberry ran a competition a few years ago to find the oldest of their coats still in existence and an 1896 garment won. *That* represents value for money. The basic formula, therefore, that can be applied to whether or not something is financially worthwhile, is: *original cost* divided by *times worn*.

There are some areas in which it is advisable not to skimp – shoes and handbag, for instance. In other cases you really can save. A glance at the fashion pages of national daily papers might suggest that all 'everyday dresses' are in the three-figure bracket. This is simply not true. Cleverly chosen dresses from some chain stores can look at least four times their real cost.

Cosmopolitan – the magazine whose fashion pages influence women of all ages – told me categorically that 'classics, and good quality clothes, may initially seem expensive but often last the longest'.

93 *Investment dressing – a good Burberry raincoat can be worn more or less anywhere, anytime, and therefore the 'original cost' divided by 'times worn' makes this a worthwhile investment (make-up by Lancôme, photograph courtesy the Inter-Continental Hotel, London).*

94 *Perhaps you could buy a suit at a more reasonable cost . . . but this Aquascutum pure new wool outfit immediately indicates its quality by, for instance, stripes exactly matching on pockets/front and collar/front, and by the inclusion of in-seam pockets. It is elements like these that increase the investment value of a garment (courtesy Aquascutum).*

Mistakes

Everyone makes mistakes. The important thing is to realize when these have been made – and perhaps 'pass on' the offending garment (see ideas on selling clothes, p. 109).

And – *try not to repeat mistakes!*

95 *At other times sheer luxury can result in an outfit of such beauty and quality that you do not even begin to compute the 'cost per wearing' (courtesy AnnaBelinda).*

Saving money

Saving on clothes can be accomplished by ingenious planning of the basic wardrobe. The more versatile the garments, the more outfits you will have from the basic ingredients. Following the 'value for money' principle will also in the long run save money. Other suggestions for saving money on basic clothes include:

(**a**) Shrewd shopping.

(**b**) Borrow from friends (a good idea for outfits for special occasions).

(**c**) Make your own (see chapter 15).

(**d**) Sell your discards.

Selling discards

Since there is no point in hanging on to clothes unless you are quite sure you will wear them one day in the distant future, you will save a lot of valuable storage space and probably make a little money if you sell your unwanteds.

Ways of disposing of discarded clothes include:

1 A sale at a friend's house, preferably not right near you. Ask the friend to publicize the sale. Give her a good percentage of all money taken.

2 A charity shop, again preferably outside your home area. You can get lists of nearby shops from the relevant local appeals' office.

3 As with buying clothes secondhand (see next chapter), you can find suitable nearly new and similar shops and dress agencies through whom to sell by looking in the Yellow Pages.

CHAPTER 14

Shopping

First, let us look at the alternative ways to get hold of the right clothes for your life.

Mail-order

Shopping in the privacy of your own home is time-saving in that you can choose your favourite garments while you stir the hollandaise sauce. It can also be money-saving in that you are spared petrol or bus fares in getting to the shops and you might also avoid extra spur-of-the-moment buys.

The disadvantages of shopping by post include the delay in receiving your goods. It sometimes seems that many services offering mail-order fashion do not actually manufacture the garments until they are requested, and certainly more time elapses than the stated '14 days' delivery' that accompanies the advertisement. This extra delay is especially apparent when you order one-offs advertised in a magazine or newspaper.

To protect yourself, before you send off a coupon from such an advertisement:

1 Make sure that the title and date of the publication is written on the advertisement.

2 Make a note of the number of the cheque, money order or method of charge payment you authorized.

3 Keep the advertisement, and make sure that the name and address of the people to whom you sent the ordering coupon is on the advertisement, as well as on the coupon you cut out to send.

4 Make a note in your diary, say after the '14 days' delivery' advertised, to remind you to check on whether the goods have arrived.

If you are dissatisfied with the long delay in delivery, you can contact the advertiser concerned. If you are still dissatisfied, write to the magazine or newspaper where the advertisement appeared, enclosing a photocopy (xerox) of the advertisement).

Delays can be a nuisance. There is one women's magazine which has most attractive 'special of the month' offers to which I have often been tempted. On each occasion the required black evening trousers, for instance, arrived long, long after the Christmas season was over, or the warm leisure jumpsuit was finally delivered when we were right into the middle of a freak British summer. I am now strong-minded enough not to be enticed by any more offers in that publication.

You are generally less likely to have problems if you order from a specific mail-order catalogue. If you do not have access to such a catalogue, look for advertisements in magazines. Send off for one catalogue – although you may find that you are soon on the regular mailing list for several other publications, too, and that can really be a nuisance.

If you have an account with a big department store (see p. 128), it is convenient to be able to mail order from them. Some of the best stores even publish their own 'magazines', which are, in effect, mail-order catalogues. The *Harrods'* magazine is a supreme example: it can be purchased through news-stands in Britain for about the same price as an expensive 'glossy', but it is automatically sent, free, to all account customers, even if they have not ordered anything recently!

Budget shopping
by Diana May

A successful way of dressing well on limited means is to scour either specialist shops that sell seconds and ends-of-lines (this includes factories' own warehouse shops like Reldan's); or second-

96 *Budget shopping from British Home Stores.*

hand shops; or shops that do both, side by side; and even what the Americans call 'thrift shops' (charity shops like Oxfam, Help the Aged, the Home Farm Trust, etc.). This is becoming a more upmarket thing to do, which means there tend to be nicer things and more of them – but you will have to check regularly and choose unerringly, as there is no going back for a different size or colour.

A good way to find such places convenient to you is to check the columns of your local paper, to read the small ads in newsagents' windows, or to consult the Yellow Pages ('Dress Agencies').

Check everything *very* carefully while you are in the shop. Remember that if you buy a skirt with a torn seam, you cannot go back and complain if you bought second-hand or discount. If you find a fault when you are checking a garment in shop, determine whether you are competent enough at sewing to rectify the fault. Be wary of soiled garments unless you are a whizz with stains (see p. 128 in 'Clothes care', chapter 16). Faults in the actual fabric of the garment may be difficult to hide.

Designer clothes at half the original retail price can be bought at factory outlets in Britain and the USA – and, especially, in Hong Kong. If you are away from home, ask the concierge of your hotel where to go. Check local papers, advertisements in shop windows, etc.

You can also have fun buying seconds at 'hostess parties' – but beware of the legal responsibilities if you are the hostess (see *Complete Woman's Reference Book*, Penguin).

Second hand clothes shops can be marvellous hunting grounds, especially if they are not so near to home that you are likely to end up with your neighbour's cast-offs!

These shops tend to such memorable names as 'Nu-2-U', 'Pass-On', 'Odds 'n' Togs' and the eternal 'Nearly New'... we went to visit one such shop, Switchgear of Windsor. They sell garments from sizes 8 to 18, and Janet Emerson says that many of her regular customers call in three or four times a week to see what might just have come in.

Department stores

One of these days, I would like to write a book about the outstanding department stores of the world (Harrods, Neiman-Marcus, Bloomingdale's, KdV, Stockmann's, Wako and so on . . .).

For the busy, discerning person, the advantage of having an account at, say, Harrods, is multifold. You automatically get their beautiful catalogue free. You can order through the mail – and if anything goes wrong they bend over backwards to help. (On one occasion I had a box of quarter bottles of house champagne sent to a friend: the package arrived damaged and was more than amply replaced.)

On the other side of the Atlantic, the Neiman-Marcus stores cleverly accept only their inhouse card – and no charge cards. I was sent to the beauty parlour in their store in the Galleria, Houston, to have a disastrous hair colouring repaired. Gary Gooding did a great job in putting my hair to rights, but when I came to pay I did not have enough cash and they would not accept my charge cards. 'No problem,' I was told, 'you can open an account with us in five minutes.' Within that time, sure enough, I had my Neiman-Marcus account and now I can shop at their stores throughout Texas and in California, Washington, Florida, Boston, Chicago and Las Vegas.

On a more local level, many people have their own favourite department store which sells everything from candles to candlewick bedspreads, and underwear to umbrellas.

Most of these shops started out as small family-run stores which were later taken over by such bigger organizations as Debenhams or House of Fraser.

I went to visit one such important local department store in Britain.

Dingles of Dorchester is very much just that – it is part of the Dingles division of the House of Fraser but to its loyal staff and to customers it is 'the Dorchester shop'. There has been trading on this site, in the county town of Dorset, since 1784. Dingles of Dorchester today sells nearly everything the shopper needs, other than food and drink. If there is enough demand for something not already on sale it will be made available – a picture department has recently been added, for instance. There is special attention to the younger shopper and also those who are older: Wednesday, when local buses bring in people from all around the county, is an especially good day, and many people come and shop then.

An important consideration at Dingles is that shopping should be *fun*; there are often live or video promotions in the shop, and twice a year there is a public fashion show. The main catchment area is within 25 miles and delivery is generally free within this area. Shoppers from further afield can often get goods sent from Dingles to another store in the group. The young manager, Les Byard, has a team of 55 full and part-time colleagues, only five of whom are men. Each of the four floors has a DSM (Department Sales Manager) and they liaise together so that if you are shopping on one floor the DSM can advise you how to co-ordinate, say, a coat, with a bag from another floor. Shopping cards make multi-purchases easier – you have to pick up your goods from the accounts department on the second floor, but there is a lift and someone – even the manager – will always help you carry them down.

Because it is a small staff there is tremendous enthusiasm and good service. The manager receives telephone calls and letters from satisfied customers, and pins them on to the staff notice board, which generates friendly rivalry between departments. There is a staff incentive scheme and good pension facilities, and they also receive discount and special fashion and make-up advice.

Haute couture

Who actually buys *haute couture*? I have been travelling extensively recently, working on an international guide for business men and women—and I am surprised at how many automatically turn to name designers first of all.

Obviously jetset names and royalty (Candy Spelling of *Dynasty* fame, Nancy Kissinger and HM Queen Noor, to name but three) buy from couture houses. And so, too, do some of those Middle Eastern princesses who have designer clothes made up in special outsized versions.

But well dressed *ordinary* people, especially in Europe, learn the value of investing in something really special—an Yves St Laurent day dress that will 'go anywhere', a Missoni all-purpose silk.

Europeans have to spend a lot of money anyway on clothes, however basic. They have the intelligence to spend just a little bit more on something that will look even better and probably give longer service.

How to shop

So, there are the alternatives, although they are generalizations, and it really depends where in the world you live. In the United States, for instance, retailers have realized for years that success comes from knowing the market and serving it, which means there are many more highly successful specialist shops aimed at, for instance, the career woman, or the younger person who loves garish T-shirts.

Wherever you shop, try not to wait until the last moment when you need something so badly that you buy badly, in desperation.

Let us return to that chic land of France. As Martine Borgemeister says:

> I do not wait to buy until I *need* something. I do a lot of window shopping and buy when I find something that really catches my eye. Since I dress in Reims I go around the name stores first: Daniel Hechter, Yves St Laurent, Cacharel, Courrèges and the like. If I do not find something there, then I go to the more expensive shops who sell a variety of model clothes.

(That, of course, is a big national difference ... a Frenchwoman 'checking out' designers' own shops before going to a more general store!)

Avoid mistakes

'I am never forced into buying something,' says Martine, 'either by the shopkeeper, or a close friend, or by the man of the moment. I only buy if I think I look and feel good and comfortable, then, to make sure, I get a second opinion.'

And, whenever and wherever you shop, remember that you need to check each garment for:

1 Fit

2 Colour.

3 Suitability for purpose (e.g. a *silk* boilersuit?).

4 Quality of dressmaking (checks matching, is the garment lined, are buttons sewn on properly?).

5 Washing instructions.

Fit

At some points in costume history (e.g. the 1950s) tight-waisted garments supposedly emphasized the wearers' figures, but in fact made them aware of their second helping of cheesecake or apple pie. Today, fortunately, the trend is increasingly away from *having* to exaggerate our figures.

The importance of keeping your body in shape and taut regardless of what size you are overall is mentioned in the 'Body style' chapter (2).

What I want to reiterate here is the fact that when you have put clothes on *you should not be aware of them.* Once you sense that a sweater is too tight or that you cannot bend over in your jeans, you subconsciously will not feel, and therefore look, nearly so good.

A few points to remember at all times include:

(**a**) Unless you have a stunning figure, too-tight clothes look cheap (and I use that in the American sense of the word!).

(**b**) Sizings in different garments vary. Just because you usually wear, say, a size 8, you must not automatically buy a size 8 without trying it on.

(**c**) No-one but you will know that the garment you are wearing is a size 10 rather than your usual size 8.

(**d**) Generally, less expensive garments are cut less generously than their more expensive counterparts.

(**e**) If in doubt, *buy big.*

Help

To save shopping for yourself, you might consider going to a 'shopping service'.

Fashion advisors help you *save* money by making fewer mistakes. They help you put together the wardrobe that is best for your lifestyle.

Wally Rogers, a Texan in her late thirties and with an extrovert teenage son, is one of the most comfortably elegant women I know. With a training in home economics and many years'

experience in fashion retailing, she started Fashion by Appointment to help others get maximum enjoyment from their clothes with minimum expense of time and money.

Wally says it is important to put together the look that is right for *you.* Some of her personal clients want help in compiling a budget wardrobe for a first job in a big city, while others want regular updating of professional wardrobes. Some people want help as they lose weight – or gain – and others need a lightweight set of clothes for a cruise, or a special dress for a party.

Wally physically checks every item in someone's wardrobe.

> I tell people to get rid of something for a particular reason – I do not just say 'get rid of it'. I make sure I have exhausted each possibility of what *could* be done with a garment. I say, 'This is a wonderful fabric, let's take the top off, make it into a strapless dress and put a jacket over it.'
>
> I think it is the selection of clothes that is important, not the money that is spent. Time and thought and planning your wardrobe are where it all starts. First thing, everybody should have a folio in which to collect thoughts, cuttings, pictures. Take time to think. Are you still influenced by your mother's fashion?
>
> Take every receipt for what you spend over three months or six months – including shoes, tights etc. – and at the end of the time work out if you are happy with your look.

While Fashion by Appointment can put together an entire wardrobe for you, others offer specific help with shopping – if you live, for instance, overseas or in the country. One such organization, Finders Seekers, charges a flat 10% on any amount they spend on your behalf. They deliver free of charge to a London hotel, or they will dispatch worldwide.

CHAPTER 15

Make your own

Dressmakers

If you have no idea what you need but you want someone to design and make a single outfit, or an entire wardrobe, for you, think of someone like Su Quek.

Su trained at the Katinka School in London and can interpret your own special needs be they for a wedding gown for a six-footer or a travel wardrobe for a fifty-year-old. She will send you sketches and swatches and, if you accept the quotation, supply finished garments.

If you have your own designs but cannot transpose them into finished garments, or if you want something really special, you need a dressmaker.

The best way to find an everyday dressmaker, who can 'run up little dresses' and do alterations and the like, is to look in your Yellow Pages or the advertisements in a newsagent's window, or to ask friends if they have such a treasure they will share.

If you want a couture dressmaker, you might have to look at the advertisements in a glossy magazine.

One such dressmaker is Gerald Kane of London. He can work to your ideas – or he can provide his own – and complete a garment in 2 to 3 weeks, or less if you are in a hurry. Even if you provide your own material, it will cost you well over a hundred pounds even to have a day dress made by him, but you are assured of a couture garment that is made specially for you.

Is it worth it to make your own?

At times it has been less expensive to make your own clothes than to buy ready-made but today, with so many attractive garments available extremely reasonably, you might not find it economical to make your own. High labour costs in some parts of the world preclude the use of custom dressmakers: in other areas dressmakers charge little but their results sometimes look decidedly amateur (see 'Around the world', chapter 12).

My advice is that, in general, it does not make sense to sew for yourself unless you really enjoy it and/or you need it as therapy, or unless you are a non-standard shape.

Before attempting to make an outfit, consider the following points.

1 How much would it cost to buy ready made?

2 How much would it cost to make? Include:

(*a*) all the materials, including pattern, fabric, buttons, zips, lining and threads;

(*b*) approximate labour costs – number of hours you would take to make the garment multiplied by a realistic cost per hour;

(*c*) depreciation cost on your sewing machine;

(*d*) electricity.

Then ask yourself:

3 Would it really be less expensive to make?

4 Are you a good enough dressmaker? (If you are *not*, and would like to be, see 'Learning how to sew', p. 118.)

5 Would you wear the garment when it is finished?

I can speak from experience in this matter. Years ago I did actually start out studying fashion design and I made all my own clothes. It got to the stage, however, where, as my life became increasingly busy, I used to make clothes in too much of a hurry. I made an embarrassing number of mistakes – many of which my clever sisters fortunately used to be able to alter into something that was actually wearable.

Remember the maxim that while *handmade* is something admirable when it comes to good dressing, *homemade* is anathema, and should be left to the world of cakes and biscuits!

There are, of course, occasions when home dressmaking is the most economical and satisfactory solution to a problem.

1 Perhaps you have a shirt of a particular red and you cannot find a matching skirt anywhere. It makes sense, if you *can* find exactly the right shade of fabric, to make a skirt.

2 Similarly, if you have a lot of time on your hands – say you are housebound with a broken leg – then whiling away the hours making a complicated beaded jacket would be a viable proposition.

Alterations

A knowledge of home dressmaking is also essential when it comes to updating last year's styles, or when other alterations are required.

98 *Alterations and updating galore ... take a T-shirt and remove one shoulder, or make a vertical cut of about 1.5cm at one side seam and knot the ends, or cut away most of the T-shirt and wear it over another, or cut two T-shirts in half vertically and join them together, or join the T-shirt to a gathered skirt to produce a dress ...*

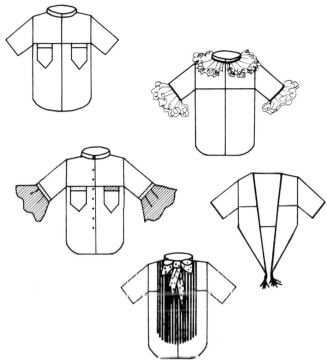

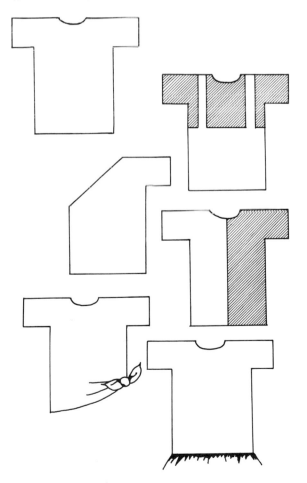

99 *More ideas, with a plain white shirt. Add lace collar and cuffs, coloured cuffs, ribbon sewn on to produce an evening shirt effect, or cut the collar and bottom off, add black piping and tassels and make a short 'jacket'.*

100 *Long trousers can be shortened ... and shortened ... and put back together again (thought: why not have one leg longer than the other?).*

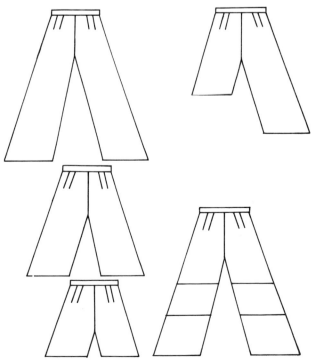

You can personalize a plain white shirt, for instance, by adding coloured pockets or lace cuffs. You can take a basic dirndl skirt pattern and give it frills or pockets.

Learning how to sew

If you are lucky enough to have access to video tapes of some of Ann Ladbury's television programmes, you can pick up all sorts of tips – and her books cater for everyone, from the beginner who barely knows how to thread a needle, through to the advanced dressmaker who wants to know many different ways of putting in invisible zips.

Ann does quite a lot of promotions around the country, and has her own range of dressmaking products to help you achieve the professional touch.

Suggested further reading: Ann Ladbury, *The Dressmaker's Dictionary* and *Weekend Wardrobe*, Batsford.

Supplies

I personally love my Frister + Rossmann machine, so it made sense to ask Sally Ormston, on behalf of that company, what to look for when buying a new machine.

There are still one or two hand-operated models available at very cheap prices. Otherwise, modern sewing machines are electrically operated and fall into four main categories:

Straight stitch machines sew only in a straight line and the majority will also sew in reverse to reinforce and finish seams. They come with some accessories and are in the lower price bracket.

Plain zigzag machines, as well as doing straight stitching forward and reverse, have a needle which swings from side to side to produce zigzag stitches for tidying the raw edges of seams, appliqué work, embroidery, and satin stitching. They can also make buttonholes (not automatically) and sew on buttons. They come with a variety of accessories, and prices depend on the machine's capabilities.

Semi-automatic and *fully automatic* machines usually incorporate all the above plus automatic mending stitch, blind hemming and fancy hem stitch, and sometimes semi-automatic buttonholing. The fully automatic versions go even further – they make buttonholes automatically and have a wide range of special practical and decorative stitches, including ones for sewing modern stretch and knitted fabrics – called stretch stitches. If you are keen on embroidery, there are machines which have numerous cams or discs which are simply dropped

into place to produce beautiful automatic patterns. Here again, prices vary according to what the machines can do.

The most recent development is the *electronic* machine, first introduced in 1976. It has an electronic 'brain' which replaces some of the mechanical parts, and, simply by pressing a button, any one of the many different stitch patterns is instantly available. These are the most expensive of all the machines.

Fabrics

It is always worth buying *good quality* fabric.

Here are some guidelines to suitable fabrics (supplied by *Pins & Needles* magazine):

1 For coats, jackets, suits, straight skirts or tailored dresses – corduroy, crisp silks, firm jersey cotton, flannel, gaberdine, tweeds, wools.

2 For blouses, full skirts, soft dresses – soft falling fabrics such as batiste, crêpe, laces, lawns, soft sheers, fine wools.

3 For dresses and skirts in straight and pleated styles – crisp, firmly woven fabrics such as linens, wool mixes, polyester blends.

4 For dresses, tops and skirts for evening wear – crisp fabrics such as organza, taffeta, wild silk and slinky fabrics such as chiffon, crêpe, fine satin, silk or synthetic jersey, silky velvets.

Fabric conversion chart

Fabric widths

90 cm = 36 in.
100 cm = 39 in.
114 cm = 45 in.
140 cm = 52 in.
150 cm = 60 in.

Fabric lengths

0.10 m = $\frac{1}{8}$ yard
0.21 m = $\frac{1}{4}$ yard
0.42 m = $\frac{1}{2}$ yard
0.63 m = $\frac{3}{4}$ yard
0.95 m = 1 yard
1.85 m = 2 yards
2.75 m = 3 yards
3.70 m = 4 yards
4.60 m = 5 yards

101 *It is always worth buying good fabric – this is a silk jacquard from the Elegance mail order catalogue (design by* **Kazazian,** *photograph courtesy Elegance).*

Other techniques

Crochet tops worn with fabric skirts ... knitted panels let into a blouse top ... embroidered yokes to nightdresses ... mixed-media dressing really looks good!

Dyeing

Dyeing can give a new lease of life to an old garment, and since it is quite difficult to find anyone today to do your dyeing professionally, it makes sense to do it yourself.

Dyeing can be used to change part or all of the colour of plain fabric, and it can also produce drastic effects for knitting, crochet and other techniques (see some of the colour illustrations of mixed-media dyeing by college students).

You cannot dye darker things to lighter shades without first using a colour remover. Neither can you successfully dye acrylics and those with drip–dry finishes.

Here are some useful hints from Dylon for successful use of their dyes:

1 Read all instructions supplied with the dye.

2 Check the type of fabric first for (*a*) the correct dye and (*b*) shrinkage.

102 *Crocheted waistcoat specially designed by Twilleys of Stamford (instructions are available from Mary Gostelow).*

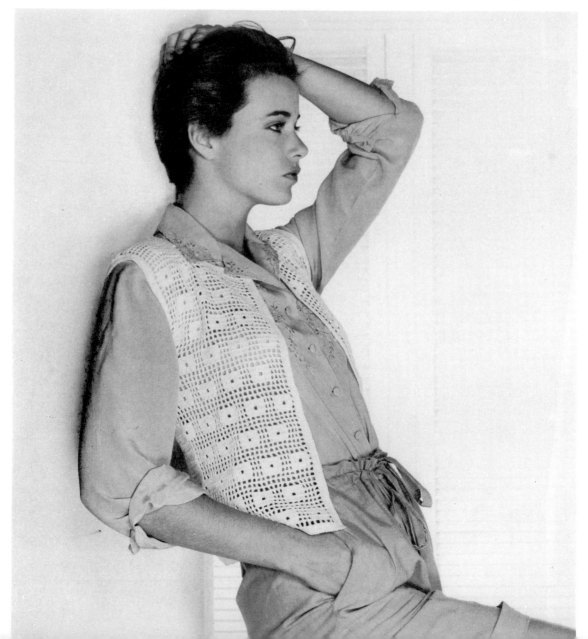

103 *Dyed dress, designed and made by Alexandra Buglass of Ravensbourne College of Art for a Dylon competition (hair and make-up by Rebecca at Pierre Alexander, shoes by* *Bally, photograph by Eamon J. McCabe, courtesy Dylon International).*

3 Weigh fabric before purchasing dyes, as successful colour results depend on using the correct amount of dye for the fabric, based on a certain amount of dry fabric.

4 Wash new articles to remove dressing. Dye cannot evenly penetrate dressing, nor can it penetrate a waterproof, drip-dry or similar finish.

5 Remove all dirt and stains prior to dyeing.

6 Use a vessel large enough to contain sufficient water completely to cover the fabric and allow for easy manipulation.

7 Wet fabric thoroughly before putting it into most dye solutions.

8 Rinse fabric thoroughly after dyeing. Wash separately if non-fast dyes are used.

Here are some of the main faults in home dyeing (and prevention ideas – in parentheses – supplied by Dylon).

1 Patchy results:
(*a*) insufficient manipulation (stir article continually);

(*b*) dye vessel not large enough (use a big enough dye bath);

(*c*) article not wet thoroughly (saturate article thoroughly prior to dyeing).

2 Reduced colour:
(*a*) incorrect water temperatures, in the case of hot water dyes (you should allow water to reach boiling point, then simmer for full dyeing time – do not treat polyester above 60°C);

(*b*) not enough dye (weigh articles dry and use correct amount of dye to weight of fabric);

(*c*) stated amount of salt and soda not added to a cold dye (read instructions carefully).

3 Uneven absorption of dye:
(*a*) dye prevented from penetration by a dressing or special finish on the fabric (if suitable, boil fabric with detergent to remove dressing; if finish cannot be removed, do not dye).

4 Over-concentration of colour:
(*a*) too much dye has been used (remember to weigh articles dry and use correct proportion of dye by mixing the dye powder in a 1pt calibrated jug using only the correct proportion – e.g. if dyeing 4oz material and using a tin of dye formulated for $\frac{1}{2}$lb of fabric, use only $\frac{1}{2}$pt of the dye solution.

5 Little or no penetration of colour:
(*a*) this type of fabric is unsuitable for dyeing (remember you cannot dye acrylic);

(*b*) you have selected the wrong type of dye (use the correct dye for your fabric);

(*c*) heavy finish, as, for instance, on drip-dry or waterproof fabric (you should not dye fabrics with special finishes).

6 Incorrect colour:
(*a*) original colour was not an even, light colour, free of stains – or your dye blended with your basic colour (you can pre-treat your fabric with a special product to remove colour and provide an even base for the new colour).

(See *Fabric dyes* booklet, full of useful hints, from Dylon – address at back of book.)

Embroidery

Zandra Rhodes and Bill Gibb regularly incorporate embroidered embellishment into their *haute couture* clothes. Another talented designer who has made a special name for her exquisitely embellished garments is Belinda O'Hanlon, who started AnnaBelinda with a friend when they were studying in Oxford some years ago.

AnnaBelinda gowns are dreamy medieval creations just right for today's world. Wedding dresses, dance dresses and everyday dresses are often highlighted with, for instance, quilted or embroidered panels.

Belinda produces professionally. Many skilled needlewomen are themselves, however, similarly embellishing their clothing with embroidery.

I first met Kay Doty in California about ten years ago. Today her marvellous 'fabric collage' jackets are highly prized collectors' items, and she has been honoured at many important exhibitions. Each jacket is a kaleidoscope of different fabrics, carefully pieced together, quilted and embellished. Many are completely reversible.

If you want to commission someone to make an embroidered item for you, you could contact one of the embroiderers' guilds (addresses at back of book).

104 *This sumptuous dress, designed by Belinda O'Hanlon, has special-effect neckline and sleeves and embroidered bands (courtesy AnnaBelinda).*

Knitting

Many couture designers – Bill Blass, for instance – co-ordinate knitted items with fabric garments. The concept of a 'jersey' does not necessarily entail partnership with a tweed skirt. For a bit of variety, try pairing a long cotton sweater with a mid-calf satin skirt for an unusual evening look.

Have you ever longed to knit such a designer sweater? If so, several designers sell kits that come complete with all yarns, buttons if required, and full instructions. You simply provide needles – and time. It will probably cost you less, however, to put together your own patterns and yarns.

The least expensive method of knitting is to 'make' your own yarn. At one time I simply tore 5 yards of calico into lengthwise strips $\frac{3}{4}$in. wide, knotted them, and knitted them. I have now come across a much easier method.

Take a rotary cutter *with guide arm* (this is important). Take also a square of fabric, say 40 × 40in. Set the guide arm to your required 'yarn width', say $\frac{1}{4}$in. Start cutting diagonally

105 *Knitted cap and scarf specially designed by Twilleys of Stamford (instructions are available from Mary Gostelow).*

across one corner of fabric. At the appropriate point *before* you reach the edge of the fabric, turn the knife through 180° and come back, almost to that edge of the fabric, and so on. This way you will end up with a joined series of S-shaped strips of the exact required width. If you like, you can cut off the corners of the S-bends.

(Rotary cutters should be generally available. If you want to check on your nearest supplier, contact the Olfa Corporation, address at the end of the book.)

You can also knit your own accessories. Twilleys of Stamford have designed, specially for *Dress Sense*, a top in their Stalite yarn, a knitted hat and scarf in their Capricorn bulky – and a crochet waistcoat using their Lyscordet. (You can get all three patterns, free, by contacting Mary Gostelow Enterprises.)

CHAPTER 16

Clothes care

Basic care

The only way to describe basic clothes care is to preach.

It takes only a couple of seconds to hang up something, or fold it up carefully. It takes minutes (if not more) to press that same item, or take it to be dry-cleaned.

Fold sweaters carefully. Apart from thick jacket-type garments, it is always better to put them away folded and flat, rather than hanging like a coat.

Never put away used underwear, even temporarily. You will forget about it until you come to wear it again.

Grandmother may always have used shoe trees and she had a point. A single pair of the new absorbent trees, regularly put into shoes the moment you take them off and left there for a couple of hours until the shoes dry, will help to keep their shape, as well as absorbing some of the moisture from your feet.

Try to be meticulous about going through your wardrobe regularly at the beginning of each season. Similarly, be ruthless in sorting through underwear drawers on a regular basis.

Storage

As the maxim says, 'a little thought pays good dividends'. It costs only a few pounds to invest in some clothes hangers, and this expenditure will, in the long run, save clothes wear and tear.

Good plastic hangers are long-lasting and easy-care. I buy mine at Woolworth's in several colours. From time to time I try to be organized so that all blouses hang, for instance, on white hangers, but invariably I do not have enough hangers to stick to this, so the colour coding breaks down.

Avoid the thin metal hangers that cleaners often use. As Wally Rogers says: 'Metal hangers affect the shape of the garment, and if people use them for a long time and the garments are "bagged" they rust. I have seen the oxidization process occur even when the hanger is covered in paper.'

Many professional clothes storage people dislike multi-purpose skirts and trousers hangers (the type that have several bars, one beneath the other). David Eason, President of Closets and Spaces, says that such a hanger becomes too heavy and cumbersome to pull out so you have to push everything over to get to the clothes on it.

It really pays to have separate hangers for each skirt or pair of trousers. Some people prefer to hang them from loops suspended from hooked or ordinary hangers; others find the snap-close hangers easier.

The best means of storage I have found for out-of-season clothes is strong lidded cardboard boxes with clear plastic ends, so that you can see what is within (otherwise, to be honest, one labelled 'winter clothes' may easily contain summer clothes!). Mothballs, though unglamorous, are sometimes essential too.

A workable wardrobe is a timesaving investment

All too often there is far too much wasted space in a wardrobe.

Try dividing your clothes into:

1 Full-length.
2 Below-knee length.
3 Half-length (e.g. blouses or skirts).

Ideally, for maximum utilization of space you need bars hanging at three different heights, although if, like me, you never wear long dresses, you can dispense with that category – and, if necessary, drape your full-length kaftan over a hanger.

The longest garment in each of your categories

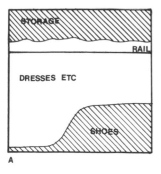 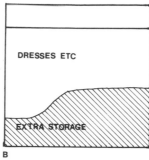

106 *Wardrobe (closet) allocations:*
A. After long and short dresses and coats are accommodated, there is space for storage above (perhaps for a shelf for sweaters), and below (perhaps for shoes).
B. Here, there is no space for storage above the clothes on the rail, but there is extra space below.

should have about six inches between it and the floor.

One of the best investments we ever made was having a carpenter build an L-shaped double wardrobe in an awkward corner of our bedroom.

I took ordinary graph paper, pencil and ruler. I measured my clothes, the height of my highest-heeled shoes, and the height of my cardboard storage boxes holding out-of-season clothes.

One facet of the wardrobe, facing the door, with double mirrored doors, has a rail to hold half-length (i.e. my longest day-length skirt plus six inches). Below are two shelves for shoes and boxed storage. Above are shelves for handbags (one) and sweaters (two).

The other facet of the wardrobe, with draw curtain for easy manoeuvring, has two upper shelves for boxed storage and, beneath, the area is divided vertically. One half holds day-length garments, and because these vary from below-knee garments to mid-calf coats, there is space for boots beneath. Under this area is a single shelf for shoes. The other half of the wardrobe holds matching separates and has three shelves for shoes beneath.

Do you separate matching separates?
Perhaps, rather like a marriage, some pairs of separates also have personality 'on their own'.

I am rather cautious and tend to hang pairs together. More adventurous dressers like Wally Rogers try to 'break them up' and hang them separately, thus suggesting other combinations.

Fabrics and how to wash them
(see 'Stains' and 'International textile care labelling code', p. 127).

Here are some guides to what fabrics are and how to care for them, from expert dressmaker Ann Ladbury:

Acetate – a cellulose fibre formed by dissolving short cotton fibres or wood in chemicals. It has a low rate of absorbency and does not conduct heat well, so garments can be warm in winter and cool in summer. Melts and burns easily. *Washing*: wash often in warm water; do not wring as creases can be permanent if the fibre cracks. Iron on wrong side with a medium iron and damp cloth or steam iron.

Acrylic – a synthetic fabric widely available, made from at least 85% of acrylonitrile, a liquid derivative of oil refining and coal carbonization. Has a fairly low rate of absorbency and is moderately flammable. *Washing*: now washes well in warm water (earlier examples tended to stretch); avoid wringing. If ironing is necessary, use a cool iron – take care, especially on jersey fabrics, to avoid stretching when pressing.

Cotton – fibre extracted from the boll or seed pod of the cotton plants. Egyptian and Sea Island fibres are generally longest, and preferable. Fabric is smooth, soft to wear, absorbent and very strong. It is flammable and creases easily unless specially treated. *Washing*: hard-wearing, so it can be washed frequently. White cotton can be bleached and boiled. Iron slightly damp with a hot iron until quite dry. (NB. Do not leave cotton damp as it is subject to mildew.)

Linen – fibre from the stem of the flax plant. Fabric strong and highly absorbent: it is a good conductor of heat, so it feels cool to the touch. It creases and burns easily. *Washing*: wash regularly, sometimes bleaching white linen. Iron fabric while evenly damp with a hot iron.

Polyamide – a synthetic fibre more commonly known as nylon, strong and highly elastic, not very absorbent so it accumulates static electricity and dries fast. It melts but does not burn. *Washing*: nylon attracts dirt particles so you should wash often. Rinse in fabric softener to prevent static electricity. Wash white and light-coloured nylons separately as they may pick up tints from other fabrics. Little or no ironing (with a cool iron).

Polyester – a synthetic fibre formed from petroleum and other chemicals, strong, resilient and with a low moisture absorbency, so it accumulates static electricity and dries fast. It melts but does not burn. *Washing*: as for polyamide (above) but if necessary use a *warm* iron.

Silk (see p. 46).

Triacetate – similar to acetate, but the final processing of the chemical flakes differs to produce a more lustrous fibre with the same characteristics as acetate. *Washing*: wash often in warm water but do not wring or squeeze as the fibres can crack. It almost drips dry: press while damp on the wrong side with a warm iron.

Viscose (formerly known as rayon) – a cellulosic fibre produced by making sheets of cellulose from wood or cotton and soaking them in caustic alkali. Fibre often dull in texture, fairly strong and feels soft, cool and limp, burns easily. *Washing*: warm water, iron when slightly damp with a medium-hot iron.

For further information on fabric properties, see Ann Ladbury, *Sewing*, Mitchell Beazley.

Washing

Before you attempt to do *any* laundry, check each garment's label.

International Textile Care Labelling Code

This is intended to provide in standard form the most effective advice for fabric care for the majority of fibres and finishes in current use. It is based on five symbols, each of which is variable. The outline symbols are:

1 Washtub: washing instructions.
2 Triangle: bleaching instructions.
3 Iron: ironing instructions.
4 Circle: dry-cleaning instructions.
5 Square: drying instructions.

Wash tub: The washing process

Triangle: Chlorine bleaching

Iron: Ironing

Circle: Dry cleaning

Square: Drying

What the Code looks like

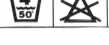	MACHINE	HAND WASH
	Hand-hot medium wash	Hand-hot
	Cold rinse. Short spin or drip-dry	
	DO NOT USE CHLORINE BLEACH	
	WARM	
	DRY CLEANABLE	
	TUMBLE DRYING BENEFICIAL	

	MACHINE	HAND WASH	
	Very hot to boil maximum wash / Spin or wring	Hand-hot or boil	White cotton and linen articles without special finishes
	Hot / Spin or wring	Hand-hot	Cotton, linen or viscose articles without special finishes where colours are fast at 60°C
	Hot medium wash / Cold rinse. Short spin or drip-dry	Hand-hot	White nylon; white polyester/cotton mixtures
	Hand-hot medium wash / Cold rinse. Short spin or drip-dry	Hand-hot	Coloured nylon; polyester; cotton and viscose articles with special finishes; acrylic/cotton mixtures; coloured polyester/cotton mixtures
	Warm maximum wash / Spin or wring	Warm	Cotton, linen or viscose articles where colours are fast at 40°C, but not at 60°C
	Warm minimum wash / Cold rinse. Short spin. Do not wring	Warm	Acrylics; acetate and triacetate, including mixtures with wool; polyester/wool blends
	Warm minimum wash / Spin. Do not hand wring	Warm / Do not rub	Wool, including blankets and wool mixtures with cotton or viscose; silk
	Cool minimum wash / Cold rinse. Short spin. Do not wring	Cool	Silk and printed acetate fabrics with colours not fast at 40°C
	Very hot to boil minimum wash / Drip-dry	Hand-hot or boil	Cotton articles with special finishes capable of being boiled but requiring drip drying
		HAND WASH	Articles which must not be machine washed. Details will vary because garment manufacturers are free to put their own written instructions on this label
			Do not wash

 This symbol indicates that household (chlorine) bleach could be used. Care must be taken to follow the manufacturer's instructions.

When this symbol appears on a label household bleach must *not* be used.

There are four variations of the ironing symbol. The first three have dots to indicate variations in temperature and the fourth, the symbol crossed out, indicates that the article should not be ironed. The temperatures shown in brackets are the maximum sole plate temperatures indicated by the dots in the symbol.

 HOT (210°C) Cotton, linen, viscose or modified viscose.

 WARM (160°C) Polyester mixtures, wool.

 COOL (120°C) Acrylic, nylon, acetate, triacetate, polyester.

 DO NOT IRON. (This symbol should only be used in cases where ironing would be detrimental to the fabric and NOT on easy care fabrics to indicate that ironing is not necessary.)

DRY CLEANING

 There are also variables which apply to the dry cleaning process, but normally these are not controlled by the owner of the goods to be cleaned. The exception only exists for those using coin operated dry cleaning machines, who should check that the cleaning symbol shown on the label is the same as that in the instructions given on the front of the machine.

Ⓐ Normal goods dry cleanable in all solvents.

Ⓟ Normal goods dry cleanable in perchloroethylene, white spirit, Solvent 113 and Solvent 11.

Ⓟ Goods sensitive to dry cleaning which may be cleaned with the same solvents shown for Ⓟ but with a strict limitation on the addition of water during cleaning and/or certain restrictions concerning mechanical action or drying temperature or both.

Ⓕ Normal goods dry cleanable in white spirit and Solvent 113.

Ⓕ Goods sensitive to dry cleaning which may be cleaned with the same solvents shown for Ⓕ but with a strict limitation on the addition of water during cleaning and/or certain restrictions concerning mechanical action or drying temperature or both.

 Do not dry clean. The cross must be of the shape shown overlying the circle.

 Tumble drying beneficial.

Do not tumble dry.

Dry-cleaning

Your dry-cleaner offers a whole range of services, besides clothes care:

1 Household – curtains, blankets, loose covers, rugs, etc.

2 Suede and leather (see p. 43).

3 Repairs and alterations: if you are losing weight fast, for instance, take your now-too-large clothes to be taken in professionally.

4 Express service.

5 Flame- and showerproofing.

6 Dyeing.

7 Some dry-cleaners will store your clothes while you move house or are away: Jeeves of Belgravia, for instance, have branches both sides of the Atlantic and provide a nationwide mail-order service.

8 For information on dry-cleaning, contact the Dry-Cleaning Information Bureau (address at end of book).

Stains
by Diana May

Notes
1 Read and learn *before* spills happen (some of these tips will apply not only to mishaps on clothes but to stains on carpets, upholstery, etc).

2 See 'International textile care labelling code,' p. 127.

General rules
1 When a spillage occurs, act quickly, but only after thinking carefully. Set-in stains are much harder to remove *but*, if you take the wrong action, you may make matters worse. At table, for instance, never dab a food stain with a coloured paper napkin, or you may have its colours to remove as well.

2 Remove the garment to be cleaned, if you are still wearing it.

3 Always prepare yourself before tackling a stain. Put an apron on, and rubber gloves to protect your hands from chemicals (you don't want your bright red nail varnish coming off on the stain you are trying to remove).

4 Always have a set of stain removal aids to hand – see 'Stain removal first-aid box', p. 129. It helps if you have some idea of the properties of different stain removers before you have to use them, and some idea of the strength that should be used. Please remember to keep all stain-removers out of reach of toddlers and pets, and make sure they are all well labelled.

5 Never use cleaning fluids in an unventilated area or near a naked flame.

6 Check the effect of the chemical first on an unimportant piece of the garment's fabric (e.g. the inside of the hem).

7 Ensure that any solid matter – e.g. ice-cream, egg, make-up and worse – that has not actually entered the material is scraped off carefully first with a clean knife or spoon. Try not to push more into the garment as you do this.

8 Any cleaning should be done with a wad of cotton wool and kitchen roll underneath, to absorb the stains going out that way. (NB. Do not use your kitchen J-cloth, as it may have grease on it.)

9 Act on the wrong side of the stain, thereby pushing the stain out from the way it entered.

10 Start by encircling the stain by a ring or irregular star-shape of cleaning fluid and working *inwards*. This avoids the indelible ring you get when working outwards.

11 If in doubt, use cold water before trying other things you have to hand: do not use hot water or soap as they might set the stain irretrievably.

12 On old-set stains, or those that involve heavy staining like lipstick, try to 'float' the stain out first with glycerine, eucalyptus oil, petroleum jelly (Vaseline) or even clean salad oil (which will, when they have done their job – after some time, in the case of set-in stains – simply wash out along with the stain).

13 It is common sense to try weaker solutions of gentler products before stronger solutions of tougher ones.

14 Finish every stain-removal exercise by hand-washing and rinsing the garment in cool water with rinse aid.

15 In your household or recipe file, or whatever is most accessible, maintain a section into which you put all swing-tags from new garments which detail special washing instructions (make sure you will remember which swing-tag describes which item).

16 Always try to buy clothes that are easy-care, preferably washable and non-iron.

Stain removal first-aid box

Have as many of the following items grouped handily together, maybe in a box with a carry handle. Keep the box in a place that is safe from junior members of the family but known to all adults and easily accessible to them.

Make sure that all bottles of chemicals, especially non-proprietary brands that you buy much more economically from your pharmacist, are well labelled.

Here is a suggested list of your box's contents, followed by an explanation. (NB. You will probably feel you only need one of each alternative.)

Dry cleaning fluid (DCF) or material: (*a*) bought as carbon tetrachloride, Beaucaire or Dabitoff in liquid form; (*b*) bought in aerosol form such as K2r or Goddard's Dry Clean; (*c*) a piece of white chalk or talcum powder.

White methylated spirit or surgical spirit (which is just meths with small quantities of castor oil and wintergreen added).

Ammonia or laundry borax or bicarbonate of soda (baking powder) or washing soda.

White vinegar (acetic acid) or acetone or amylacetate or nail varnish remover (see caution below).

White spirit or turpentine.

Mild bleach such as hydrogen peroxide or 'hypo' (sodium thiosulphate) or sodium perborate. (NB. Household bleach, hypochlorite or chloride bleach, is really too strong except for the toughest whites.)

Movol or oxalic acid, a special bleach that removes iron mould and rust.

Glycerine, eucalyptus oil, petroleum jelly or salad oil.

Copydex latex adhesive remover (see Copydex tube for details).

Biological enzyme detergents (Ariel or Biotex).

Frend or Shout pre-wash spray.

Lighter fuel.

Old clean toothbrush or nail brush.

Comb (to use as mini-washboard).

Though you obviously will not keep it permanently in your kit, rely on a soda syphon or a bottle of soda water (in the US, 'club soda'), as an ally in the cleaning war. A strong squirt of it as soon after the calamity as possible should flush out many liquid stains, especially wine, and neutralize nasty smells (as does white vinegar, when you are cleaning up animal and human messes).

There is now a useful range of specialist cleaning liquids on the market called Stain Devils, with different cleaners for different jobs. An accompanying leaflet tells you which Stain Devil to use for what.

To return to your own ready-assembled – and cheaper – kit, here are suggested strengths of use of each, with some idea of their action (note, however, that, tried and tested as these have been, each stain is a different problem, as it varies in content and intensity on different materials, so ultimately the responsibility is yours alone).

Remember: if you are nervous about a stain, do not delay about taking it to the cleaners and pointing it out to them, explaining what the stain is.

(NB. *Numbers* refer to symbols on chart below.)

Carbon tetrachloride (*1*) is a grease-solvent cleaning fluid that you can obtain more cheaply from your local pharmacy counter than if you buy it in a commercial bottle with a pad on top (the pad gets dirty the first time you use it and, on all subsequent uses, may add more dirt than it removes). Use direct, working inwards. It is useful for removing sticky marks from price labels. Do remember that, like most of the chemicals mentioned, this is poisonous: it can harm the skin and it releases toxic fumes, so it is best used in the open air. It is also harmful to rubber and acetates. The aerosol cans of dry-cleaning spray are good, though in an emergency talcum powder, french chalk, fuller's earth or a piece of chalk (for collars) will do.

White, methylated or surgical spirits (*2*) are also good grease solvents, toxic and flammable. They dissolve oil, varnish, ballpoint and some paint. They can be warmed, never directly but in a container of previously heated water, for maximum efficiency. Use directly, or diluted 50% with great care on rayons or acetates. Like lighter fuel, they will remove Elastoplast marks. Meths damages rayon and tricel.

Glycerine (*3*) and other jellyish things are in your box to help 'float' out stains, as explained in the general rules.

All *acetones* (*4*), which are good grease and lacquer solvents, must be treated with great respect, especially working near plastic surfaces, which they affect, and on such modern synthetic fibres as acetates, tricel and rayon. Amylacetate or lighter fuel *may* be all right on them, but the stronger acetone and nail varnish remover will not, so be assiduous about testing a corner first on any modern fabric whose origins you are not sure of. If in doubt, use white vinegar (acetic acid), and always dilute heavily.

Turpentine and *white spirit* (*5*) will probably be in your toolshed already as paint thinners. They are good for grease- and resin-based stains, tar, polish and oil-based paint. When real turps is stipulated, do not use substitute. Use directly, but remember that it is flammable and not suitable for acetate and triacetate fabrics.

Ammonia and *borax* (*6*) are alkalis that neutralize acids and help dissolve grease. Cloudy ammonia, the strongest, is a liquid that must be diluted 3 times by water (or about 1tbs to ½pt water). It is toxic, caustic and harmful to skin, eyes and mouth – but it is efficient. Borax is much safer, taking the form of crystals which can be used as water softeners, or as a pre-wash soak. It is safe with most fabrics. Use ½oz crystals to 1pt warm water. Washing soda (sodium carbonate) is also useful for pre-wash soaking, but keep it away from aluminium saucepans, and wool and silk. Baking soda can be used neat on acid stains (lemon juice and so on), then flushed with cold water.

Mild bleaches (*7*) are useful for removing the colouring matter left by stains. They must be used with caution, and never on drip-dry or crease-resistant fabrics, nylon, wool and silk. Hydrogen peroxide is easily obtained from the chemist and should be used 1pt to 4 parts of water. Soak non-fast colours for 30 minutes and whites for 12 hours, and then rinse well. 'Hypo' (sodium thiosulphate) and sodium perborate are quite mild and may be used (both 1tsp to 1pt water) with caution on most materials, even wool.

Movol (see other ideas, in brackets in the chart on p. 131) is to remove iron-mould and rust, and *Targon* is self-explanatory. In an emergency – say a picnic on the beach – *butter* will shift tar.

Enzyme detergents (*8*), with their 'biological' action, are there to tackle 'biological' stains, that is, protein stains such as blood, egg, milk and sweat. They may affect non-fast colours, flame-resistant or rubberized fabrics, metal fastenings, rayon, silk or wool (use Woolite for wool). Perhaps their great virtue is that they have introduced the current generation of housewives, used to instant results, to the virtues of soaking, be it in detergent, salt water, or just cold water. Always soak in a plastic bowl or bucket – a metal one could leave iron stains.

Specific stains

This list of suggested action is merely a guide to generally accepted solutions. Where there are alternatives, try the milder solution first and then rinse thoroughly before trying another (some of these chemicals react badly to each other). If, say, glycerine *and* carbon tetrachloride are offered as cures, use carbon tetrachloride on the fresh stain and use glycerine to loosen up an old stain which you might later remove with the carbon tetrachloride.

If you have read this chapter carefully (rather than just turning to it in a panic when a disaster has happened!) you should know enough about the general principles of cleaning to use your common sense about what and how much to use. Good luck!

Table of stain removal

Suggested attention

1 DCF
2 meths or surgical spirit
3 glycerine
4 white vinegar or acetone
5 white spirit
6 ammonia or borax
7 mild bleach
8 biological detergent
* Stain Devil available
(other suggestions in brackets)

acid, battery 6
adhesives
  clear or contact 4 * (or washing-up liquid, lighter fuel)
  latex 4 (or Copydex remover)
  'super glue' (own remover)
beer 2, 4, 7 * (or soda water)
beetroot 6 (borax soak) *
bird droppings 8 * (cold salt water)
bleach (hypo)
blood 6, 7, 8 * (cold salt water)
brandy * (K2r)
butter 1, 8 * (K2r)
caramel *
carbon paper 1, 2 *
chewing gum 1, 2 * (pick off ice-cooled solids first)
chocolate 1, 6 (borax soak) 8 *
Coca cola 1, 7, 8 *
cod liver oil 1 *

coffee 1, 3, 6 (borax soak) 7 *
cosmetics 1, 3, 6 (brief ammonia) 8 (K2r spray)
crayons 1 *
creosote 1, 3, 5 (or try coal-tar naptha)
deodorant 4, 6 *
duplicator correcting fluid 2, 4
egg 8 * (cold salt water)
Elastoplast 1, 4 (lighter fuel)
faeces 4 (white vinegar) 6 (borax soak) 8 (or soda water)
fruit juice 3, 6, 7, 8 (dry starch)
grass 2, 3 *
gravy 1, 8 * (cold water)
grease 1, 8 * (K2r spray or sprinkle talcum powder and rub off)
hair spray 2 *
ice cream 1, 8 *
indelible pencil 2
ink
  ballpoint 2, 4 * (or the tip of a booklet match)
  felt tip 1, 2 *
  washable, dried * (Movol)
iodine 6, 7 *
iron mould * (Movol, lemon juice * salt, eucalyptus oil or even salad oil)
jam 6 (borax soak) 7, 8 *
lipstick 1, 3, 8 *
mascara 1, 2, 3 *
mayonnaise 1, 8
metal polish 5
mildew 7 * (or mild disinfectant)
milk/cream 1, 6, 8 * (or soda water)
mud, engrained 2
mustard 1, 2 *
nail varnish 2, 4 * (or nail varnish remover)
nicotine 7
oils 1 *
paint
  emulsion * (cold water)
  gloss 4, 5 * (commercial paint remover, Polyclens)
paraffin and petrol 1 (K2r)
perfume 3, 4 *
perspiration 4, 6, 7, 8 *
plasticine 1
polish
  car *
  furniture *
  metal 1
  shoe 1, 6 *
  wax 1, 2, 5 *
resin *
rust * (lemon juice or Movol)

salt water *2*

sauces and ketchups *3, 7, 8* *

scorch *3, 6* (borax soak) *7*

seaweed *2*

soot *1*

spices *6* *

spinach *2, 3, 8*

spirits (gin etc.) *7, 8* *

starch *8*

tar *1, 2, 3, 5* * (butter, or try coal-tar naptha or eucalyptus oil)

tea *6* (borax soak) *7, 8*

treacle *

typewriter ribbon *1, 5* *

urine *4, 6, 8* * (soda water)

varnish *2, 4* *

Vaseline *1*

vegetables *

vomit *4, 6, 8* (soda water)

wax, candle and sealing *1, 2* * (iron, first, with brown paper)

wine *3, 6* (borax soak) *7* * (soda water – or, in emergency, pour white wine on red wine)

Speedy repairs

Here are some cover-ups until something can be repaired:

1 If a zip breaks, cross-stitch it until you have time to put in a replacement.

2 If a zip is difficult to open, rub the teeth with a lead pencil.

3 If a hem starts coming down, use adhesive tape, staples or safety pins.

4 If a button pulls off, leaving a hole, bend a paperclip through the button and, bent at right angles, through to the back of the hole (disastrous for the fabric, but such first aid might be necessary for the moment).

If you need something invisibly mended, ask your dry cleaner and/or look in the Yellow Pages.

CHAPTER 17

The future

A few people always want to be wearing not only the latest thing, but even tomorrow's style. The rest of us simply want not to look as if we are perpetuating last year's fashion.

How do you keep up to date?

Reading glossy magazines gives a good indication of the extremes from which one or two modified trends can be adapted. Some of these magazines deliberately photograph garments as if to make them, and those wearing them, look as ugly as possible. I have also heard people remark that all the fashion pages in newspapers make clothes look really unattractive: the model might be sitting, for instance, with her legs wide apart, her hair might be deliberately tousled and she may hold a cigarette in hands adorned with chipped nail-varnish.

It seems to me that fashion editors do not generally expect people to look like the models in the photographs. Illustrations are used to exaggerate a point. The badly groomed model, for instance, is probably wearing a skirt that has so much fullness to it that it *could* be worn with legs wide apart. From a profusion of illustrated ideas, a general message is intended.

The exception is provided by *Women's Wear Daily* (usually known as *WWD*), the trade's mentor as to what is going to happen. More accessible to the general public is the gloriously illustrated full-colour newspaper called simply *W* (USA and Japan), *B* (Hong Kong) and *Mode* (Australia).

For details, and subscription rates, either contact the headquarters of your local edition or send a large stamped addressed envelope to Fairchild Publications (address on p. 140).

If you want to keep abreast, you should look at as many magazines and papers as you can. Check through some that are intended for other age groups. Look in as many different ethnic publications as possible.

Watch what people are actually wearing. Notice little details on clothes worn by newscasters and other television personalities. What are the Royal trendsetters – the Princess of Wales and Princess Michael of Kent, and American born Queen Noor of Jordan, wearing? Check colours, skirt lengths, padded or non-padded shoulders, waisted or non-waisted.

Look in shops that feature new designers, and try to go to as many fashion shows as you can. If your local art school has a display of students' work, go along to see what the designers of a few years' hence are producing.

Look to the future

What is going to happen in the future? Remember Iwan Tirta's comment, that soon we shall all be wearing tubes . . .

Listen to another designer, James Ferreira: 'Dressing is certainly going to become more casual, with the American influence becoming more pronounced. At the same time, cutting will become more imaginative. Garments will be sleek, with clean lines, and able to be worn by every age.'

I asked Cyril Kern where he thought fashion was going: 'With the progression of modernism and the possible blandness of environmental surroundings, the contrast of life could be in "exotic dressing".'

Sheridan Barnett, one of Britain's top designers, feels that there could be a renaissance of traditional clothes, highly decorated 'almost in revolt against the emptiness of modernism.'

I personally believe that clothes will become more *fun* to wear. Malcolm McLaren, a trendsetter in both fashion and rock music, predicts that fashion will increasingly be 'the way you're going to announce yourself. It's all about having a good time.'

Padded Yoke;

Cotton Satin Seams & pkted Dress.

Back Button Collar;

slit;

Straight across seamed dress worn with or without Sash

V inseamed pkts

James Ferreira

107 *Comfort and ease remain necessary requirements of the future. This James Ferreira design has a wide expanse of straight-down fabric held with a comfortable waist sash; there is plenty of room for the arms to 'move'.*

108 *International outfit with Japanese influence was designed and made by Susan Watts of Ravensbourne College of Art (hair and make-up by Rebecca at Pierre Alexander, shoes by Bally, photography by Eamon J. McCabe, courtesy Dylon International).*

This is certainly the message from the Japanese, from designers like Rei Kawakubo (Comme des Garçons) and Yohji Yamamoto (Y). As Takeo Hosaka, bureau manager of the Paris branch of Seibu department store, says, 'Japanese don't think of just fashion. They think about life as a whole – culture, habits, nature, just like a writer.'

Not everyone can wear Japanese clothes literally, but most can accommodate a degree of the freedom that these garments give the wearer. I love my Japanese clothes: everything seems to be able to worn in so many different ways – upside down, inside out, and so on. Each wearing expresses my mood of the moment.

And that is what dressing is all about. It enhances the mood – your personality.

Happy dressing!

WEIGHTS AND PERSONAL RECORDS

Weights

The Flora Project for Heart Disease Prevention
suggests the following ideal weights. Note:

1 These weights are without any clothes on.

2 If you are under 25 (and over 18) subtract
1lb ($\frac{1}{2}$kg) for each year under 25.

height ft in (cm)	small frame lb (kg)	medium frame lb (kg)	large frame lb (kg)
4 10 (147)	96–104 (44–47)	101–113 (46–51)	109–125 (49–57)
4 11 (150)	99–107 (45–48)	104–116 (47–53)	112–128 (51–58)
5 0 (152)	102 110 (46–50)	107–119 (48–54)	115–131 (52–59)
5 1 (155)	105–113 (48–51)	110–122 (50–55)	118–134 (53–60)
5 2 (157)	108–116 (49–53)	113–126 (51–57)	121–138 (55–63)
5 3 (160)	111–119 (50–54)	116–130 (53–59)	125–142 (57–64)
5 4 (163)	114–123 (52–56)	120–135 (54–61)	129–136 (58–66)
5 5 (165)	118–127 (53–58)	124–139 (56–63)	133–150 (60–68)
5 6 (168)	122–131 (55–59)	128–143 (58–65)	137–154 (62 70)
5 7 (170)	126–135 (57 61)	132–147 (60–67)	141–158 (64–72)
5 8 (173)	130–140 (59–63)	136–151 (62–69)	145–163 (66–74)
5 9 (175)	134–144 (61–65)	140–155 (63–70)	149–168 (68–76)
5 10 (178)	138–148 (63–67)	144–159 (65–72)	153–173 (69–78)

Standard body measurements
(*British Standards Institution BS3666:1982*)

(inches in brackets)

standard bust measurements

8	78–82	(31–32)
10	82–86	(32–34)
12	86–90	(34–35$\frac{1}{2}$)
14	90–94	(35$\frac{1}{2}$–37)
16	95–99	(37$\frac{1}{2}$–39)

standard hip measurements

8	83–87	(32$\frac{1}{2}$–34)
10	87–91	(34–36)
12	91–95	(36–39$\frac{1}{2}$)
14	95–99	(37$\frac{1}{2}$–39)
16	100–104	(39–41)

Fashion sizes

British	American	German	French
10	8	34	38
12	10	36	40
14	12	38	42
16	14	40	44
18	16	42	46

Shoes sizes

British	3	4	5	6	7	8	9
Continental	$35\frac{1}{2}$	$36\frac{1}{2}$	38	$39\frac{1}{2}$	$40\frac{1}{2}$	42	43
American	$4\frac{1}{2}$	$5\frac{1}{2}$	$6\frac{1}{2}$	$7\frac{1}{2}$	$8\frac{1}{2}$	$9\frac{1}{2}$	$10\frac{1}{2}$

Tights and stockings sizes

British	8	$8\frac{1}{2}$	9	$9\frac{1}{2}$	10	$10\frac{1}{2}$	11
Continental	35	36	37	38	39	40	41

(American, same as British from $8\frac{1}{2}$ up)

Your sizes and favourites

Personal measurements
Height

(metric)	(feet and inches)
....	....

Weight

(date)	(kilos)	(pounds)	(stones)
....	....	....	....

Measurements:
Private measurement notes (see how to measure yourself correctly in How *you* can do it, chapter 3).

My measurements are:

1 Bust (around its most obvious part) ....

2 Waist ....

3 Hip (5in. down from waist)   ....

4 Hip (9in. down from waist)   ....

5 Sleeve length (from natural shoulder to wrist, arm extended)   ....

6 Upper arm   ....

7 Wrist   ....

8 Back shoulder width at nape of neck ....

9 Back length, nape of neck to waist   ....

10 Back length, waist to usual hem   ....

11 Neck   ....

My sizes are:

bras ....

(styles to remember ....)
dresses ....
(styles to remember ....)
shoes.............................
(styles to remember ....)
skirts..............................
(styles to remember ....)
tights ....
(styles to remember ....)

shopping details to remember:

(date)	(place	(shop)	(details)
....	....	....	....

SUGGESTED FURTHER READING

Here are some general books that Diana May and I have found particularly helpful:

Jack Angell, ed., *Lingerie: original designs for you to make*, David and Charles

Oleda Baker, *How to renovate yourself from head to toe*, Futura

Sandra Barwick, *A century of style*, Allen and Unwin

Susan Bixter, *The professional image: the total program for marketing yourself visually – by America's top corporate image consultant*, Putnam

Emily Cho and Linda Glover, *Looking terrific*, Ballantine, New York

Emily Cho and Hermine Lueders, *Looking, working, living terrific 24 hours a day*, Ballantine, New York

Maria da Conceiçao, *Exquisite clothes to make and treasure*, Mills and Boon

Christina Ferrare DeLorean and Sherry Suib Cohen, *Style: how to have it in every part of your life*, Simon & Schuster

Leah Feldon, *Dressing rich: a guide to classic chic for women with more taste than money*, Pedigree

Kate Hogg, *More dash than cash*, Hutchinson

Carole Jackson, *Colour me beautiful*, Piatkus

Brigid Keenan, *Dior*, Octopus

Frances Kennett, *Secrets of the couturiers*, Orbis

Jan Leeming, *Simply looking good*, Arthur Barker

John Molloy, *Dress for success*, Foulsham

Kaori O'Connor, *Creative dressing: the unique collection of top designer looks that you can make yourself*, Routledge and Kegan Paul

USEFUL ADDRESSES

At the risk of seeming like a biased directory, here are names and addresses of people specifically mentioned in this book who have something to offer by correspondence – or whom you may want to contact for further details of items illustrated.

AnnaBelinda
6 Gloucester Street
Oxford OX1 2BN, GB

Body Focus (Danskin Press Office)
Barbara Attenborough Associates
1 Harewood Place
London W1R 0PQ, GB

British Crafts Council
43 Earlham Street
London WC2H 9LD, GB

British Home Stores
Marylebone House
129-137 Marylebone Road
London NW1 5QD, GB

Career Guild
6412 Vapor Lane
Niles
Il 60648, USA

Chrissy G
Fabricmead Ltd
PO Box 72
Reading
Berks RG1 8PL, GB

Color Me Beautiful
PO Box 3241
Falls Church
VA 22043, USA

Colour Me Beautiful
PO Box 127
London SW11 4RP, GB

David Shilling
44 Chiltern Street
London W1M 1PL, GB

Disabled Living Foundation
346 Kensington High Street
London W14 8NS, GB

Dry Cleaning Information Bureau
Lancaster Gate House
319 Pinner Road
Harrow
Middlesex HA1 4HX, GB

Dylon International Ltd
Worsley Bridge Road
London SE26 5HD, GB

Elegance Fabrics (UK)
650 Holloway Road
London N19 3NU, GB

Emanuel
26a Brook Street
London W1Y 1AE, GB

Embroiderers' Guild
41A Hampton Court Palace
East Molesey
Surrey KT8 9AU, GB

Embroiderers' Guild of America Inc
6 East 45 Street
New York
NY 10017, USA

Emily Cho
PO Box 1594
Cathedral Station
New York
NY 10025, USA

Equipment for Disabled
2 Foredown Drive
Portslade
Sussex BN4 2BB, GB

European Commission for the Promotion of
  Silk
50 Upper Brook Street
London W1Y 1PG, GB

Fairchild Publications
7 East 12th Street
New York
NY 10003, USA

Fashion by Appointment
PO Box 1870
Houston
TX 77251, USA

Fashion Extra
Bridgewater Place
Manchester M60 6AP, GB

Finders Seekers
10 Lyford Road
London SW18 3LG, GB

Harrods
Knightsbridge
London SW1X 7XL, GB

Harvey Nichols
Knightsbridge
London SW1X 7RT, GB

Hong Kong Trade Development Council
Great Eagle Centre (31/f)
23 Harbour Road
Hong Kong

International Gold Corporation
30 St George Street
London W1R 9FA, GB

International Wool Secretariat
Wool House
Carlton Gardens
London SW1Y 5AE, GB

James Ferreira
47G-Khotachiwadi
Girgaum
Bombay 400004, India

Jeeves of Belgravia
8/10 Pont Street
London SW1X 9EL, GB

John Lewis
Oxford Street
London W1A 1EX, GB

Leather Institute
Kings Park Road
Moulton Park
Northampton NN3 1JD, GB

The Limited Inc
PO Box 16528
Columbus
OH 43216, USA

Long Tall Sally
21 Chiltern Street
London W1M 1PH, GB

Marc Young International
107 Arndale Centre
Poole Dorset BH15 1SY, GB

Moss Bros
21-26 Bedford Street
London WC2E 9EQ, GB

Mothercare
Cherry Tree Road
Watford
Herts WD2 5SH, GB

Neiman-Marcus
PO Box 64780
Dallas
TX 75206, USA

Neostyle Optical
55/61 Brewery Road
London N7 9QH, GB

Olfa Corporation
Higashi-Nakamoto 2-11-8
Higashinari-ku
Osaka 537, Japan

Pearson School of Needlepoint
25 Kildare Terrace
London W2 5JT, GB

Royal Silk
Royal Plaza
45 East Madison Avenue
Clinton
NJ 07011, USA

Sassa
10a Gee's Court
London W1M 5HQ, GB

Selective Marketplace
Belton Road West
Loughborough
Leics LE11 0BR, GB

Shoe and Allied Trades Research Association
SATRA House
Rockingham Road
Kettering
Northants NN16 9JH, GB

Twilleys of Stamford
Roman Mill
Stamford
Lincs PE9 1BG, GB

Working Woman
342 Madison Avenue
New York
NY 10173, USA

Working Woman
77 Farringdon Road
London EC1M 3JY, GB

INDEX

References to illustrations are printed in *italics*